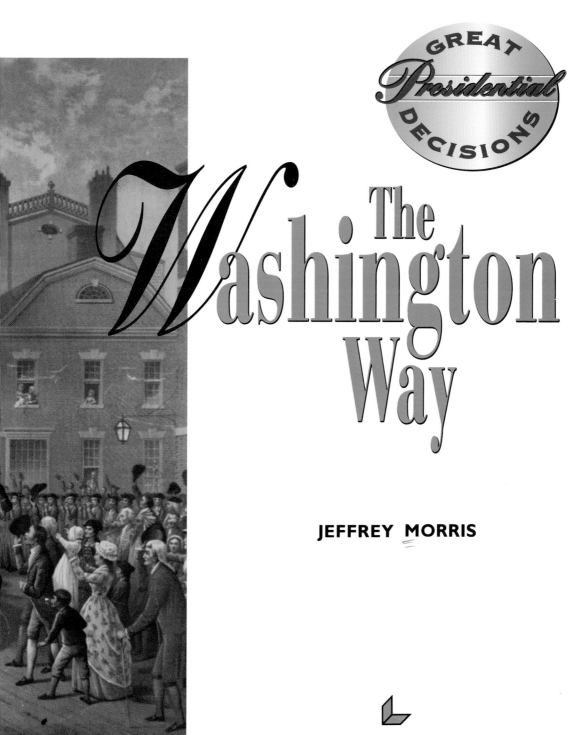

GREAT
Presidential
DECISIONS

The *W*ashington Way

JEFFREY MORRIS

LERNER PUBLICATIONS COMPANY
MINNEAPOLIS

To Lillian
with deep affection

Previous page: George Washington arrived in New York City in 1789 to become the first president of the United States.

Copyright © 1994 by Jeffrey B. Morris
Published by arrangement with Lou Reda Productions, Inc.

Library of Congress Cataloging-in-Publication Data

Morris, Jeffrey Brandon, 1941-
   The Washington way / by Jeffrey B. Morris.
     p. cm. — (Great presidential decisions)
   Includes index.
   ISBN 0-8225-2928-9
   1. Washington, George, 1732-1799—Juvenile literature. 2. United States—Politics and government—1789-1797—Decision making—Juvenile literature. I. Title. II. Series.
E312.66.M65 1994
973.4'3'092—dc20   94-10548
                                           CIP
                                           AC

Manufactured in the United States of America
1 2 3 4 5 6 – I/JR – 99 98 97 96 95 94

Contents

Introduction

*T*HE AMERICANS WHO WROTE the Constitution of the United States faced an unusual opportunity. Their country had won independence from Great Britain, which had a monarchical government. Most European nations at that time were governed by monarchies— by kings and queens. But Americans wanted a republic, a form of government in which power resides with those citizens who are entitled to vote. The government is run by elected officers and representatives who are responsible to the citizenry and who govern according to law.

The framers of the United States Constitution wanted a government powerful enough to protect the country from foreign enemies, but not powerful enough to take away the rights of the citizens. To

George Washington presided over the Constitutional Convention in Philadelphia in 1787, where he and his fellow delegates hammered out a remarkable new form of government.

We the People

accomplish this goal, they created a complicated form of government. The framers divided the powers of the new government among three branches. They thought that the least powerful branch would be the judiciary. That branch was supposed to hear and decide lawsuits, decide disputes between the U.S. government and individual states, and keep the other two branches within their constitutional powers.

The framers expected the legislative branch—the Senate and the House of Representatives—to be the most powerful. Congress was supposed to make laws, levy taxes, and choose how to spend money.

The framers of the Constitution had the most trouble agreeing on the powers of the executive branch. The head of that branch is the president. The framers wanted a president who could act speedily

The Constitution begins "We the people," showing that the American government is elected by the people and is responsible to them.

and forcefully. On the other hand, they definitely did not want someone with the powers of a king or dictator. The president would be elected for four years. He or she would be commander in chief of the military forces, would be primarily responsible for relations with other countries, and would ensure that the laws passed by Congress would be carried out. The president could also veto laws passed by Congress, but Congress could override that veto.

The framers thought that each branch of government would work at a different rate of speed, because each would have its own set of duties. They thought the judicial branch would act most slowly, partly because lawyers usually need time to gather evidence and present their cases, and because fair decisions require careful deliberation. The framers of the Constitution thought Congress would also act relatively slowly, because of the need to gather information, debate the issues, and get agreement among many members. However, the framers wanted the president to be able to act rapidly and decisively.

Delegates to the Constitutional Convention included *(left to right)* Alexander Hamilton, James Madison, Charles Cotesworth Pinckney, Benjamin Franklin, Roger Sherman, and Elbridge Gerry.

EXECUTIVE BRANCH

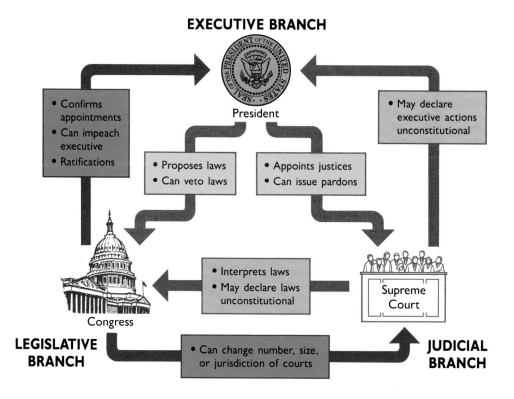

When they drafted the Constitution, the framers expected that the Supreme Court would meet at the nation's capital for only a few months each year. But they intended that the president, even when away from the capital, would act for the nation in an emergency. The framers also wanted to be sure that in some areas—such as dealing with other nations— the United States should be as unified as possible, and they hoped that the president would express that unity. For these reasons—speed, unity, and the ability to act in an emergency—the framers expected that the president would often be called upon to make important decisions.

This book is one in a series about the great decisions that some of our presidents have made. Of course, presidents make decisions every day. They decide whom to appoint to office, what to say to leaders of foreign nations, and whether or not to veto laws passed by Congress. Most of these decisions are quite ordinary. From time to time, however, the president makes a decision that will affect the American people (and often other nations as well) for many years. You may think of Abraham Lincoln's decision to free the slaves, Franklin Roosevelt's decision to fight the Great Depression, or John Kennedy's decision to fight for civil rights for African Americans. Of course, not every important decision our presidents have made has been wise. James Buchanan decided not to stop the Southern states from leaving the Union. Franklin Roosevelt decided to ask Congress to increase the size of the Supreme Court so it would more often decide cases the way he wanted. Richard Nixon decided to cover up the Watergate burglary.

This book is about the most significant decisions made by George Washington. As our first president, Washington set many precedents. The traditions he established have influenced the character of the presidency in our country and the type of government we have today. Most of his decisions worked out well. You'll find out what led to his decisions, the options he had at the time, and how he actually went about making decisions. You'll also see how his decisions were carried out and why they were important.

*B*oth the American flag and the Great Seal symbolize American values. In the Great Seal, the eagle holds both an olive branch and arrows, reminding us that the United States desires peace, but will wage war if necessary.

CHAPTER ONE

Starting Out

WASHINGTON LEARNED OF HIS election as president on April 14, 1789. Two days later, his neighbors gathered in Alexandria, Virginia, to honor him with a dinner and to say good-bye. The city's mayor made a stirring speech that ended, "Go and make a grateful people happy." Reluctant to leave private life, Washington replied, "From an aching heart, I bid you all...farewell."

Washington began the journey to his inauguration the next day. His wife, Martha, remained behind; she would follow later. The inauguration would take place in the nation's first capital, New York City. Traveling sometimes by carriage and sometimes on horseback, Washington journeyed about 250 miles in eight days.

Thousands of Americans thronged to wish Washington well as he journeyed to his inauguration. Here he enters the city of New York.

At each settlement along the way, throngs of people turned out to cheer Washington. They set off fireworks and held receptions and dinners for him. Guards of honor marched with him at times along the route. Cannon roared and church bells rang in greeting. When Washington arrived in Philadelphia, Pennsylvania, every avenue was filled with cheering people. In Trenton, New Jersey, a crowd of little girls and townswomen threw flowers to him and sang, "Welcome mighty Chief! Once more. Welcome to this grateful shore!"

At Elizabethtown, New Jersey, Washington set sail for New York on a 47-foot barge. In boat after boat, all decorated with flags, well-wishers followed him, until the parade of vessels stretched out for more than a mile. Later, one observer wrote that porpoises played around Washington's barge as it entered the harbor of New York that day. Whether or not that's true, we know that ships of many nations raised their flags and fired their guns as Washington's barge approached. On board some American vessels, choruses sang to the music we now know as "America," or "My Country 'Tis of Thee":

> *Joy to our native land*
> *Let every heart expand*
> *For Washington's at hand*
> *With glory crowned.*

Finally, Washington's barge landed at Murray's Wharf, where thousands of citizens were waiting for their new president. So ended Washington's triumphal journey—a magnificent procession unequaled in American history.

Washington as he looked on his inauguration day, April 30, 1789.

Washington's barge landed at Murray's Wharf in New York City, where both American and foreign ships saluted him with flags and guns.

Just one week later, Washington stood on the balcony of Federal Hall. He was dressed in a brown suit with buttons that displayed an eagle with outspread wings. He wore white silk stockings and silver shoe buckles, and he carried a dress sword. Before an enormous crowd, he placed his hand on a large, leather-bound Bible and took the presidential oath. At the end, he added, "So help me God," and kissed the Bible. "It is done," said Robert R. Livingston, the judge who had given him the oath.

When Washington took the oath of office, he wondered whether he could live up to the expectations of the American people.

"Long live George Washington, president of the United States."

So began the first term of our first president— with the widespread love and respect of his countrymen. At the time, Washington wondered whether he would be able to live up to the expectations of the American people. But he did prove worthy of their esteem. As president, he was true to his principles and firm in his decisions. He never forgot that he was responsible to the people. When he stepped aside after two terms as president, he made it clear that the president of the United States would not turn out to be a king.

Young George Washington

The real George Washington isn't easy to discover. Too many tall tales have grown up around him. Washington didn't chop down a cherry tree as a boy. He didn't throw a silver dollar across the Potomac River *or* the Rappahannock River (even though one of his biographers said he did). And he probably didn't stand up in a boat crossing the Delaware River during the Revolution (as a famous painting shows him). But he certainly was a great general, a great president, and a great man. Let's look at why, without being misled by all the myths about him.

Washington was born in 1732 on a plantation along the Potomac River in Westmoreland County, Virginia, about 50 miles southeast of what is now Washington, D.C. When he was three, his family moved to a plantation at Little Hunting Creek on the Potomac. Three years later, they moved again, to the Ferry Farm on the Rappahannock River near Fredericksburg, Virginia. George was the fifth child in a family of seven boys and three girls.

Washington's birthplace

George's father was Augustine Washington. His mother, Mary, was Augustine's second wife. When George was 11, his father died, leaving the family three farms. Mary Washington lived for many years after her husband, and saw her son become president (though she and George never got along very well).

Unlike most of our country's founders, George Washington never went to college. In fact, he had little schooling. His father's death meant his family couldn't afford to send him to school in Europe, as they had done for his half brother, Lawrence. George never learned to debate or speak well in public. But he was an avid reader, and he trained himself to write clearly and forcefully.

After his father's death, George lived most of the time with Lawrence, who was 14 years older than George. Lawrence was not only a brother, but also a friend and an important influence on George. When George was 20, Lawrence died. George became the manager of Mount Vernon, which Lawrence had inherited from their father. Later, after the death of Lawrence's widow, Anne Fairfax, he became its owner.

Another great influence on George was Colonel William Fairfax, the brother of Anne Fairfax, who lived near Mount Vernon. Colonel Fairfax trained George to be a surveyor. When he was 16, George made a surveying trip with Colonel Fairfax's son George to what was then called the "western country." This wild, unsettled land included the present state of West Virginia, as well as the western parts of Virginia, Maryland, and Pennsylvania. For two years, George made surveying trips to measure and map this wilderness.

George Washington, *standing*, became a surveyor when he was 16.

In addition to surveying, George also learned how to be a soldier. He may have been influenced by Lawrence, who had been in charge of training soldiers in his military district. After Lawrence's death, George became an army major and took over that responsibility.

George's knowledge of the wilderness, together with his military skills, soon brought him to the attention of Robert Dinwiddie, the governor of Virginia. Dinwiddie was looking for a man of property for an important task. Great Britain had claimed territory in much of the western country, but the French had also claimed the land. The French had built a fort, Fort Le Boeuf, in the Ohio River Valley. Though George was just 21, Dinwiddie sent him to Fort Le Boeuf with an urgent message: The French must leave.

In early November of 1753, George began his 500-mile journey with an interpreter, a guide, and several other men to help with horses and supplies. On the trip, Washington chose a site on the Ohio River for a British fort. He finally arrived at the French fort on December 11. The French received him politely, but their answer was firm. They certainly would not evacuate Fort Le Boeuf.

Washington headed for home in the dead of winter. He soon realized that his exhausted horses could no longer carry both men and supplies, so he split up his traveling party. He decided to take a single companion with him along a shortcut, an old Indian path. Carrying packs and guns, they set out through the woods on foot. They hoped to find the Allegheny River, which lay across their path, frozen over. Instead, the water had only frozen along the banks. The two men were forced to make a raft in order to cross. Midstream, the raft overturned. Nearly frozen, they spent the night on an island, and then returned to Governor Dinwiddie with the answer from the French.

Dinwiddie quickly promoted Washington and sent him west with six companies of soldiers—about 150 men—to construct a fort on the Ohio River site

Lawrence Washington was not only George's half brother, but also a great influence on him.

and to confront the French. This time Washington could expect a less polite encounter.

Washington and his men hastily erected a stockade and called it Fort Necessity. Then Washington rashly ordered a surprise attack on a small camp of French soldiers. The French retaliated by sending 700 troops to Fort Necessity. They quickly overpowered Washington's small force, compelling Washington to surrender.

Though he had lost the battle, Washington was still considered a hero for attacking the French. The British were determined to oust the French from the territory. They sent Edward Braddock, a British commander, to Virginia with orders to attack a key French post, Fort Duquesne. Washington joined Braddock as an aide. Together, they marched west in the spring of 1755 with 1,400 men. They traveled European-style, in a colorful procession of bands, banners, horses, cattle, and wagons.

As a young soldier, Washington led an attack on French soldiers camped near Fort Necessity in 1754.

Such an open display of force would have been an effective strategy in Europe, but it didn't work in America. As the British soldiers marched down the broad road they had made for themselves through the wilderness, the French and their Indian allies hid behind trees and rocks. Attacking from behind this cover, they were able to overpower Braddock's troops. They killed two-thirds of Braddock's men, and Braddock himself was killed. Washington demonstrated great bravery in the terrible battle. Four bullets pierced his clothing, and two horses were shot from under him. Miraculously unharmed, he led the survivors in retreat.

Again Washington had survived, and again he was promoted. Though just 23 years old, he was named commander in chief of all the colonial military forces of Virginia. The colonial army was under British command, however, so Washington still had to serve under a British officer.

One of Washington's first tasks was to guard Virginia's 350-mile border against invasion by the French and against attacks by Native Americans. Lacking many supplies, including adequate clothes, shoes, and gunpowder, Washington succeeded in defending this vast frontier with only a few hundred men. Finally, in 1758, he and his soldiers won an important victory when they captured Fort Duquesne.

Washington made mistakes in his early campaigns; he had even had to surrender a fort. But he had learned how to wage war in America and how to lead men. Later in 1758, when he chose to leave the army, he was Virginia's most experienced and respected native soldier. Word of his exploits had even reached Europe.

British commander Edward Braddock led his men into a disastrous ambush by French troops a few miles from Fort Duquesne.

CHAPTER TWO

Life at Mount Vernon

WASHINGTON LEFT THE ARMY AND returned to Mount Vernon. When he was 26, he married Martha Custis, one of the richest widows in Virginia. She had two children, Patsy and Jack, by her first husband, and Washington was an immensely devoted stepfather to them. George and Martha's marriage was a happy one.

For 16 years, Washington managed his sprawling plantation. He grew wheat and tobacco, raised sheep, manufactured cloth, and ran a mill. He constantly bought more land—much of it in the West. Eventually he owned several plantations in Virginia.

Like other Virginia plantation owners, Washington owned many slaves. As he grew older, however, he came to regret his dependence on slaves. He tried

Mount Vernon, Washington's beautiful and sprawling plantation, was situated along the banks of the Potomac River near the present city of Washington, D.C.

Martha Custis at 26

to treat his slaves well, refusing to sell them. He wouldn't move them from one plantation to another without their permission. In his will, he gave all of his 124 slaves their freedom. Nevertheless, like all prominent southerners of his era, Washington never called publicly for the freeing of all slaves.

A serious and diligent man, Washington still found many ways to enjoy himself. He loved to attend balls, plays, and puppet shows. He enjoyed riding horses and watching them race. Like many southern plantation owners, he hosted many visitors and travelers. In fact, Washington entertained an estimated 2,000 guests at Mount Vernon from 1768 to 1775. He also traveled widely—to the West, to the Great Dismal Swamp in southeast Virginia (where he owned land), to Annapolis, Maryland, and to New York.

The owners of Virginia's plantations were expected to run for the House of Burgesses, the elected branch of the Virginia legislature. Washington was elected to the Burgesses and took his seat on his 27th birthday. There he served with many brilliant statesmen, including Thomas Jefferson, James Madison, Patrick Henry, and George Mason.

In the 1760s, Americans began to resist paying the taxes demanded by the British Parliament. Washington was not as radical as some colonial leaders, but he had many reasons to resent the British. He disliked the way British army officers treated American officers as inferiors. When he sold tobacco from his plantations to British merchants, they paid him low prices. When he ordered cloth and farm equipment from Great Britain, he paid exorbitant prices and high freight rates. In return he got moth-eaten fabric and defective equipment. Though he was a British subject, Washington's loyalties had begun to shift. He began to think of himself not so much as an Englishman, but as an American.

By 1769 some members of the House of Burgesses were openly resisting the British. Washington became one of their leaders. He introduced several resolutions written by his neighbor, George Mason, which stated that the British could not tax Virginians. The Burgesses adopted these resolves, known as the Fairfax resolves. The resolves encouraged colonists throughout the South to question British authority.

Washington's influence in Virginia increased when he married Martha Custis; she was one of the richest widows in the state. They had a happy marriage, and Washington was a devoted stepfather to Martha's children.

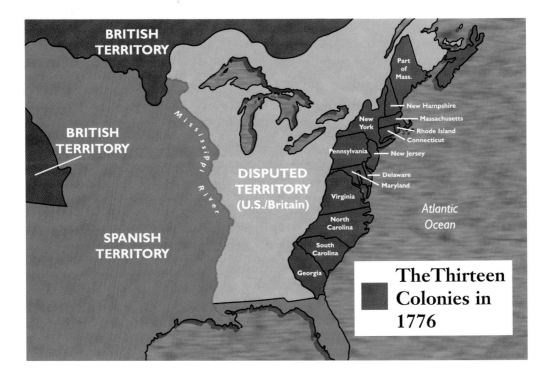

The Thirteen Colonies in 1776

Meanwhile, the British Parliament passed more laws the colonists resented. The colonists decided to work together to resist these laws. So each colony chose representatives to meet together to plan how to deal with Great Britain. These representatives met as the First Continental Congress in Philadelphia in 1774. Every colony except Georgia sent a delegate.

By this time, Washington had greatly impressed his fellow Virginians. They elected him to represent them at the Congress. In the discussion about what to do about the British, Washington argued passionately. No American government, he said, "will ever submit to the loss of those valuable rights and privileges which are essential to the happiness of every free state."

British Taxes

*D*efending the colonies from the French, Great Britain ran up a big debt. The British government thought that the colonists should pay their fair share and imposed a series of taxes on them. One of the best known was a tax on stamps. Many colonists resented these taxes bitterly. Patrick Henry *(right)* became a fiery spokesperson for the rebels, urging the colonies to unite against the British. Eventually, the colonial rebellion became the American Revolution.

It wasn't long before fighting broke out between the British and the colonists. In April of 1775, the "shot heard round the world" was fired by colonial rebels at Lexington and Concord near Boston. A Second Continental Congress met in Philadelphia in May; one of its most urgent tasks was to organize an army. Again, Washington was a delegate from Virginia.

The Congress needed to choose a commander for the new army. Since fighting had begun in New England, the Congress wanted a commander from another part of the country. They wanted to show that all the colonies supported the Revolution, not just those in New England.

Washington was the only delegate to attend

Continental Congress

olonial rebellion against the British was not well organized at first. That changed after the Boston Tea Party, when colonists dumped tea in the Boston harbor to protest British taxes on tea. The British Parliament punished the colonists for the "tea party" by closing the harbor.

In response, the colony of Virginia decided to call the colonies together to decide what to do about the British. Delegates to this meeting became known as the First Continental Congress. The Congress first met in Philadelphia on September 5, 1774. Among the delegates were George Washington, John Adams,
John Hancock, and Patrick Henry.

The Congress didn't want to make a complete break with Great Britain. Instead, it wanted to find a way to preserve liberty in America while under British rule. King George III didn't heed the attempts of the Congress to compromise, however. In fact, the British declared Massachusetts in open rebellion and forbade six colonies to trade in most parts of the world. By the time the Second Continental Congress met on May 10, 1775, the colonies were ready to go to war, and the Congress created an army. For the next six years, the Second Continental Congress spoke for the colonies and directed the war.

The Second Continental Congress

At the Second Continental Congress, John Adams proposed George Washington as commander in chief of the colonists' new army.

sessions of the Congress dressed in military uniform—a reminder of his military accomplishments. He had served on committees of the Congress that dealt with military matters, and he no doubt impressed his colleagues with his military knowledge and good judgment. Also, he was not from New England, but from the South. So it was no surprise when, on June 15, 1775, the Congress unanimously elected Washington as commander in chief of the Continental Army.

The Decision
Not to Seize Power

O N JULY 4, 1776, THE COLONIES SIGNED the Declaration of Independence. They became the United States of America, and the American Revolution was well under way. During the next seven years, Washington led the army in many bitter battles and through much hardship.

Washington's greatness as a commander can't be found in the battles he won during the Revolution. Few of his victories were significant, except those at Trenton, Princeton, and Yorktown (the final battle of the war). In fact, Washington lost more battles than he won. He couldn't hold New York. He withdrew from Philadelphia. At Germantown he was routed.

Early Americans raised liberty poles as they united to seek freedom from British rule.

At Valley Forge in the harsh winter of 1777–78, ill-equipped soldiers suffered terribly.

Yet Washington was a magnificent commander because of his clear understanding of the colonists' situation. He knew better than anyone that the British couldn't dominate America from across the wide Atlantic for long. They couldn't send enough troops to hold every important city and fort in America. Washington knew he didn't need to win all the battles. He didn't need to hold every city and fort. He only needed to hold the American army together long enough to outlast the British. If he could do that, he could win the war.

But that was a big "if." Holding the ragtag colonial army together took enormous skill. Soldiers enlisted for just one year. When the year was up, they left for home. In addition, most of them were not trained as soldiers and didn't like military discipline. To make matters worse, the army lacked many supplies. It didn't have enough guns, gunpowder, food, blankets, or clothing. Never was this more evident than during the terrible winter of 1777–1778 at Valley Forge, where starved and frozen men walked barefoot in the snow.

The Continental Army had trouble getting supplies because the Continental Congress didn't have the power to raise money. The Constitution, which now gives our Congress the right to tax, hadn't yet been written. In 1777 the Continental Congress wrote the Articles of Confederation, which outlined a loose form of government but did not include the right to tax.

So Washington had to work hard to get the Congress and the state governments to give him the men and supplies he needed. He wrote letter after letter asking for food, weapons, ammunition, blankets, horses, and pay for his troops. In fact, Washington's letters during the Revolution came to about 10,000 pages. Washington began to realize that the United States had to have a stronger central government, and it needed to be strong enough to tax, to pay its bills, and to support an army.

During the Revolution, Washington won respect from the colonists, from American allies, and even from the British. By the time the British surrendered at Yorktown, Washington was in a powerful position. Some historians think he could have set himself up then as a king. But of course he didn't. One of Washington's greatest contributions to our country was his restraint as a military leader. Granted much power by Congress, he was careful not to abuse it.

The American Revolution lasted almost eight years—touching nearly every American's life.

He would not use winning the war as a step toward taking power. He believed that in a republic, the army must always serve the people.

In 1783, the last year of the war, Washington clearly showed how strongly he believed this. After the British surrender at Yorktown, the colonies and Great Britain took two years to negotiate a peace treaty. During this time, the Continental Congress still couldn't raise the money it needed, so many soldiers were sent home without having been paid. Rightfully angry, some people—soldiers and civilians—argued that the army should use force to get

The British surrendered to Washington at Yorktown in 1783.

its wages. They said Washington should lead a military revolt. If he wouldn't, the disgruntled troops threatened to act without him.

Washington was then camped at Newburgh, New York. He called a meeting of his officers to deal with the crisis. He told them he loved his soldiers. But if the men revolted, he warned, they would take a step toward tyranny. He told them they would be acting against their own country, their own farms and property, their own wives and children.

The result might be the loss of many freedoms—freedoms the patriots had fought hard to win. Freedom of speech might be lost. Without it, Washington argued, ordinary people would be powerless. He told his officers, "Dumb and silent, we may be led, like sheep, to the slaughter."

Then Washington pulled a letter from his pocket. It was from a member of Congress, and it explained the financial problems Congress was facing. Washington wanted to read the letter to his officers, but somehow he couldn't. He looked helplessly at the paper. Finally, he pulled out something that few people knew he used—a pair of eyeglasses. "Gentlemen, you will permit me to use my spectacles," he said, "for I have not only grown gray but almost blind in the service of my country." With that, his officers wept. He had summoned their loyalty to him, and they heeded his words. The danger of military rule, the closest the United States has ever come, had passed.

By September 1783, a peace treaty had been signed. The war was over. In December, Washington attended a meeting of the Continental Congress in Annapolis, Maryland, where a special ceremony was

Washington at 40. With his vigor, honesty, and tenacity, Washington kept up patriot morale throughout the colonies during the Revolution.

Washington took warm leave of his officers after the Revolution.

planned. When it was time for him to speak, he rose and bowed. The Congressmen took their hats off to him, but they didn't return his bow. They were showing that a civilian government is a higher authority than its military.

Then Washington, his hands shaking, presented his resignation. "Having now finished the work assigned me, I retire from the greater theater of action," he said, "and bidding an affectionate farewell to this august body under whose orders I have so long acted, I here offer my commission and take leave of all employments of public life."

When Washington told the Continental Congress he was resigning as commander in chief, he set a precedent that in America the military would not try to seize political power. His decision not to make himself king was perhaps one of his greatest contributions to America.

At Newburgh, Washington had taught his officers that when an army uses force to get its way, it threatens the very freedoms it had fought to defend. When rule is by might, rather than by right, elections mean little. Later, at Annapolis, Washington showed that a great military leader could make his country free without taking power himself. Perhaps nothing in Washington's career was quite so great as his conduct at Newburgh and at Annapolis.

The Constitutional Convention

*A*FTER THE WAR, WASHINGTON returned to Mount Vernon. He had been away for a grueling eight and a half years. He relished his quiet life there, as "a private citizen on the banks of the Potomac...under the shadow of my own vine and my own fig tree." It suited his nature. "I am not only retired from all public employments," he wrote, "but I am retiring within myself and shall be able to view the solitary walk and tread the paths of private life with heartfelt satisfaction."

Though Washington had left public life, he had not really retired. By then he was probably America's largest landowner and one of its richest men. He was involved in numerous business activities. His vast Mount Vernon plantation stretched for 10 miles along the Potomac and was 4 miles wide at one point. There he supervised workers, slaves, and family—a

Washington returned to a quiet life at Mount Vernon after the Revolution, but continued to keep an eye on the new country's progress and problems.

community as large as a medium-sized town. He was an industrious, innovative planter. He put in a fruit garden, worked to develop better fertilizers, and carefully bred sheep, buffalo, and mules to produce new and superior lines.

But Washington continued to be keenly aware of his country's problems. He read newspapers, corresponded with people around the country, and talked with the many visitors to Mount Vernon. He often shared his worries about the weakness of the national government. The Articles of Confederation simply did not grant it enough power.

For example, one of the terms of the treaty of peace with Great Britain was that Americans pay the money they had owed to British merchants when

Washington and family at Mount Vernon

the war had started. The individual states would not see that this was done, however, and the national government had no power to force them. In retaliation, the British refused to evacuate forts they still occupied in American territory.

Another problem that worried Washington had to do with trade between states. Some states were discriminating against goods made in other states by taxing them. The national government had no power to regulate this practice.

Washington had become too famous a man and too concerned a citizen to be able to ignore these problems. He knew the importance of cooperation between the states from his experiences during the Revolution, when soldiers from all over the colonies fought the British together. He'd also seen the value of cooperation during his years at Mount Vernon, when he led an effort to build a canal between the Potomac River and the Ohio River. That project had required several states to work together.

Here, at the State House of Annapolis, delegates from five states decided to call a convention of all the states to revise the Articles of Confederation.

In 1785 Washington invited delegates from two states, Virginia and Maryland, to meet at Mount Vernon. This meeting led to another the following year in Annapolis, Maryland, with delegates from five states. The delegates called for a convention of all the states to improve the national government. They wanted to "render the Constitution of the Federal Government adequate to the exigencies of the Union." The Continental Congress agreed to such a convention—with one important condition. The convention was only to revise, and not to replace, the Articles of Confederation.

Washington was elected a delegate from Virginia to the Constitutional Convention, which was to be

The Articles of Confederation

The colonies adopted the Articles of Confederation in 1781. Under the Articles, the government had no executive, or head. It had no judiciary, or courts. The Articles set up only one branch of government—the Continental Congress.

But the Congress had very little power. It could wage war, make peace, and send diplomats to foreign countries. It could borrow money, but it couldn't raise money through taxes. It couldn't control commerce between states. And since the government had no courts, it could not enforce its laws.

The Articles were almost impossible to change, since amendments had to be approved by each of the 13 states. Not surprisingly, the Constitutional Convention in 1787 finally decided to replace the Articles completely.

held in Philadelphia. But he hesitated to go. He wrote, "Having happily assisted in bringing the ship into port, and having been fairly discharged, it is not my business to embark again on a sea of troubles."

At the same time, his concern about the country's weak government had grown even greater. A brief rebellion of debt-ridden farmers led by Daniel Shays in Massachusetts had deeply upset him. He wrote to Henry Knox, one of his generals in the American Revolution, saying, "There are combustibles in every State which a spark might set fire to." To another patriot, James Madison, he wrote, "No morn ever dawned more favorably than ours did and no day was ever more clouded than the present."

But once it appeared that the convention had a good chance of strengthening the government, he simply had to go. The announcement that Washington would attend had a dramatic effect on public opinion. People began to have great hopes about what might come out of the meeting.

The Constitutional Convention met for the first time on May 25, 1787, at Independence Hall in Philadelphia. So eminent were the men who attended that Thomas Jefferson called them the "assembly of demigods." Of these, Washington and Benjamin Franklin were perhaps the most respected of all.

When it came time to elect a president of the convention, the 81-year-old Franklin demonstrated his respect for Washington. He wouldn't allow his own name to be put forward, and Washington was elected unanimously. At the outset, Washington tried to inspire the delegates to set high goals. "Let us raise a standard," he is supposed to have said, "to which the wise and the honest can repair."

As president of the convention, Washington was influential throughout. Many of the delegates knew Washington from his years as commander in chief. As he spoke with them outside Independence Hall,

Washington urged the states to unite—just as Paul Revere had urged the colonies to unite in this famous engraving.

*B*enjamin Franklin stepped aside so that Washington would be named president of the Constitutional Convention.

he used his prestige, charm, and ability to tinker compromises to achieve harmony among them.

The delegates knew Washington wanted them to "probe the defects of the Constitution to the bottom, and provide radical cures." They realized the difficulties Washington had faced during the Revolution because of the lack of central power. They understood that, for Washington, the "radical cure" must be a strong central government.

The delegates decided not to simply revise the Articles of Confederation. The Virginia delegation, of which Washington was a member, offered a bold plan for an entirely new government—one with

strong central power. The Virginia Plan became the focus of the convention's attention. In the end, the delegates adopted a form of government that grew out of this plan, yet in many ways was even stronger.

The delegates set forth, or framed, this new government in the United States Constitution. It established three branches of government. To prevent any branch from becoming too strong, the framers balanced power among the three branches, and gave each branch ways to check the power of the others. With this ingenious framework, the delegates laid the groundwork for a future of both security and freedom for the new country.

Washington attended every session of the Constitutional Convention and was influential throughout. As president, all remarks were addressed to him. He reacted with anxiety to angry disagreement and with joy to compromise.

CHAPTER FIVE

Creating the Presidency and the First Election

*O*NE OF THE MOST DIFFICULT QUES-
tions faced at the Constitutional Convention
was just how much power to give the president. The framers wanted to create a strong executive,
one who could act rapidly in case of war or rebellion,
and one who could unify the young nation. But at
the same time, they didn't want to create a tyrant.

The states had written state constitutions during
the American Revolution, and these constitutions
clearly reflected a similar fear of a tyrant. Almost
without exception, these constitutions severely limited
the power of the state governors. The governors were
elected by the state legislatures, served short terms,
and were often limited to serving one term. In

A new flag, a new constitution, and a new presidency meant that
George Washington would set many important precedents.

47

addition, the governors often needed the approval of an executive council to act. They were such weak executives that some called them "little more than ciphers."

Washington's presence at the Constitutional Convention helped calm the fear of a presidency that would be too strong. Many delegates believed Washington would eventually become the first president. They trusted him. This trust encouraged them to give the president greater powers under the Constitution than they might have otherwise.

And so the framers agreed on the type of executive they wanted. He would be elected, not by Congress, but by the people. And he wouldn't depend on Congress for reelection. The president would administer and enforce the law. He would appoint the other high officials in the executive branch. He wouldn't

The Constitutional Convention was held at Independence Hall in Philadelphia.

need approval of an executive council to act. He would also serve as commander in chief of the armed forces.

But the president's powers were also checked. The president had to have the Senate's approval when appointing people to high office. He also needed the Senate's approval of treaties. Congress—not the president—was given the power to declare war. And Congress could remove the president from office through impeachment.

Despite the checks and balances, some people thought the presidency created was too strong. Thomas Jefferson worried that the president might be reelected for life. He called the presidency "a bad edition of a Polish king." Patrick Henry spoke of a "squint toward monarchy." George Clinton, the governor of New York, claimed that "if the President is possessed of ambition, he has power and time sufficient to ruin the country."

But Washington was satisfied with the office created by the Constitution. He didn't believe the president could possibly stay in power for life, like a king, unless the American people forgot to prize their freedoms. He wrote, "There cannot, in my judgment, be the least danger that the President will...ever be able to continue himself one moment in office, much less perpetuate himself in it."

For the Constitution to be adopted, 9 out of the 13 states had to ratify, or approve, it. In some of the states the vote was very close. Washington didn't campaign for the ratification of the Constitution, but the American people knew he supported it. In fact, as president of the convention, Washington had been the first framer to sign it.

Washington inspired trust, which influenced the way the presidency was set up. Delegate Pierce Butler of South Carolina wrote that the president's power would not have "been so great had not many members cast their eyes toward General Washington as President; and shaped their Ideas of the Powers to be given the President, by their opinions of his Virtues."

This parade celebrated the acceptance of the Constitution (after nine states had ratified it) in 1788.

Washington was so widely respected that opponents of the Constitution found it difficult to argue against it. Just as many delegates had thought Washington would be the first president, ordinary people began to think so too. This calmed their fears, just as it had reassured the delegates. When the Constitution was accepted, James Monroe went so far as to give Washington much of the credit. "Be assured," he wrote, "his influence carried this government."

The Decision to Accept Election

Under the Constitution, the president was to be elected by presidential electors in each state. The electors were to be chosen either by the state legislature or directly by the people. Washington did nothing to win the votes of the electors; he didn't "run" for the presidency. In fact, we have no record that he did anything at all to become president. He just didn't say he would refuse the job. Even so, on February 4, 1789, every elector voted for Washington. John Adams of Massachusetts was chosen as vice president.

Washington had mixed feelings about the election. He knew he was the likely choice. As he waited to hear the election results, he wrote, "The event which I have long dreaded, I am at least constrained to believe is now likely to happen." At 56, he knew he'd be happier managing Mount Vernon than governing a nation.

Washington also worried that he might not prove worthy of the presidency. He wrote, "I greatly fear that my countrymen will expect too much from me." He knew there would be "an Ocean of troubles." And he feared his reputation would be hurt by the mistakes he would inevitably make in office.

But Washington felt a keen sense of duty to his country. He was moved by pleadings from all over the country that no one else was as qualified for the presidency. For example, Thomas Johnson, a leading patriot from Maryland, wrote, "We cannot, Sir, do without you."

In the end, Washington was persuaded that the welfare of his country required that he give up his quiet life at Mount Vernon. When told of his election, he accepted. His sense of duty had won out over his desire for privacy and comfort. But he hoped that "at a convenient and early period" his "services might be dispensed with." He looked forward to the day he "might be permitted once more to retire, to pass an unclouded evening after the stormy day of life."

*D*elaware was the first state to ratify the Constitution; New Hampshire was the ninth. Eleven states had ratified when Washington became president. Two more—North Carolina and Rhode Island—joined shortly thereafter.

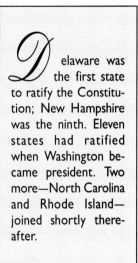

Qualities of a President

When Washington became president, he worried that he wasn't equal to the task. In his inaugural address, he spoke of himself as "inheriting inferior endowments from nature." He thought himself "unpracticed in the duties of civil administration," and "without that competency of political skills."

Certainly, Washington lacked the extraordinary range of gifts that Benjamin Franklin and Thomas

Washington's sword, *above.*

*W*ashington's inauguration on the balcony of New York's Federal Hall. From the moment he became president, Washington sought the opinions of many able advisers.

Jefferson had. He didn't have the diplomatic experience of John Jay, who had helped negotiate the treaty of peace with Great Britain. Unlike another brilliant American, Alexander Hamilton, he understood little about the country's financial problems. He was shy, uncomfortable when speaking in public, and terribly sensitive to criticism.

Though Washington may not have been as brilliant as some of his colleagues, his judgment was unmatched. He understood better than anyone what was in the best interest of his country. He was cautious in making up his mind, but once he made a decision it was usually wise. As Thomas Jefferson put it, Washington's mind was "slow in operation… but sure in conclusion."

Washington also knew how to manage people. He had the habit of command. He could surround himself with able men and listen to their advice without seeming weak. His knowledge of the nation's military problems was unrivaled. He'd learned a lot about foreign affairs during the Revolution, and he could call on John Jay, Thomas Jefferson, and others for advice about diplomacy. Though he was not a politician in the way we use the term now—he had never campaigned for office—he did have political experience. He had served for almost two decades in the House of Burgesses and the Continental Congress. He had worked with politicians while he was commander in chief, and he enjoyed friends in political life throughout the country.

Most of all, what made Washington by far the best-qualified man for president in 1789 was the enormous trust he inspired. He was respected throughout the United States—by rich and poor, by farmers, craftsmen, and tradesmen, by those who had favored the Constitution and those who had opposed it.

Washington inspired that trust because he was a man of great physical and moral courage. He embodied the best values of his generation: honor, self-discipline, impartial justice, and duty to country. He looked the part of a president—commanding, dignified, and aloof. And he conducted himself so well that his personal behavior was beyond reproach. In this, he was superior even to remarkable figures such as John Adams (who was quarrelsome), John Jay (who was a bit vain), and Thomas Jefferson (who sometimes made compromising remarks in private). With his false teeth, formal manners, and lack of ease at public speaking, Washington probably wouldn't have made a good impression on television. But for his country, in his time, his manner was perfect.

Washington had the habit of command—a quality that helped him greatly as president.

Life in 1789

*A*MERICANS FACED A GREAT QUES-
tion in 1789: Could a territory as large as
the United States be governed for long by
a government chosen by the people, rather than
one run by a king, by aristocrats, or by a dictator?
The republic Washington would head was the largest
since the Roman republic, which had ended some
1,800 years before. The United States stretched
west from the Atlantic Ocean to the Mississippi River.
It covered an area as big as Great Britain, France,
Germany, Spain, and Italy combined.

Most of that huge territory held few European
settlers. Northern New England was almost entirely without settlers; so was New York north of Albany
and west of the Hudson River. Much of Pennsylvania, western Virginia, Ohio, Indiana, and Georgia
was also wilderness. Most of America's four million

Americans worked as farmers, fishermen, shipbuilders, and trad-
ers in 1789 when Washington became president. This prosperous
farm was in Pennsylvania.

people lived within a couple of days travel of the Atlantic.

Communication was slow and difficult. America had no television, radio, magazines—or even telephones. Only a few newspapers were published (in 1784 Virginia had just one). And almost all of the newspapers reported mostly local news. Jefferson wrote in 1794, "I could not have supposed, when at Philadelphia, that so little of what was passing there could be known even at Kentucky." A letter from Philadelphia took four or five days to reach Washington at Mount Vernon, 150 miles away.

Transportation was also slow, making it even harder to unify such a vast area. Jefferson reported in March of 1790 that the roads from Richmond, Virginia, to New York City were so bad that he couldn't go more than three miles an hour. Travel could also be dangerous. One member of Congress

Stagecoaches provided the best transportation for passengers and for mail in the late 1700s.

Plantation owners in the South, who relied on slave labor, had different expectations of the new government than did the merchants and shipbuilders of the North.

died in a shipwreck while sailing to a session of Congress in 1789. Two more members of Congress almost suffered a similar fate when their ship was nearly shipwrecked. Their vessel barely made it to the coast.

Many differences divided the various sections of the young country. New England had its merchants and shipbuilders, the South held planters and slave labor, and the West was being settled by rough subsistence farmers. The people of these regions all had different expectations of the new government. Americans also came from varying ethnic backgrounds. Some were French, German, Dutch, or Swedish. A majority came from the British Isles, but even they had differences—they were English, Scotch, or Irish. How could a small, new government unite all these people and create a sense of national identity?

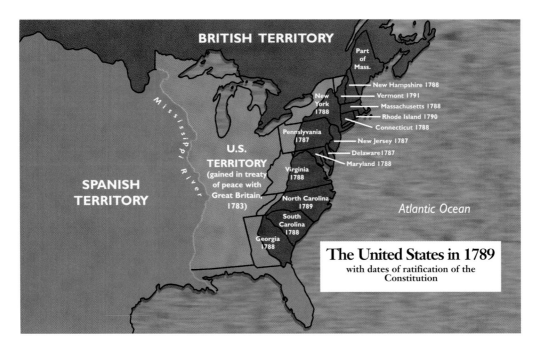

The United States in 1789

with dates of ratification of the Constitution

The World in 1789

And the new country was sorely in need of money. When Washington became president, the United States treasury was empty, yet the country's debts (many of them from the war) were staggering. And the government still had no way to collect taxes.

America also faced military threats. On the seas, United States ships were harassed by pirates. In the West, Native Americans were ready for war. Foreign nations posed a danger too. British troops were stationed on the Canadian border. They still occupied forts in New York and Michigan, even though they had promised to leave when the American Revolution ended. Spain occupied land on the southern and southwestern borders of the country. Spain also controlled the Mississippi River—a waterway Americans

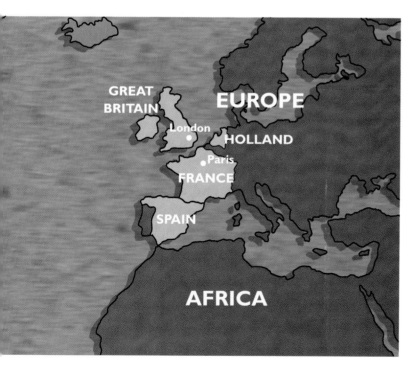

The vast and fertile lands of early America held rich resources, such as the timber on this newly cleared farm.

in the West desperately needed to ship their goods to the rest of America or to Europe. America had little with which to face these threats. In 1789 its tiny army had just 672 soldiers, and it had no navy.

One great power did appear to be friendly to the United States in 1789—France. Though the colonists had fought for the British against the French before the Revolution, the French had helped the colonists during the Revolution. In 1778, France and the United States had signed a treaty which made them allies. The validity of the treaty was in doubt, however, since it had been made by the French monarchy, which collapsed as the French Revolution began in 1789.

Still, America had great assets when Washington became president. Its rivers and streams teemed with salmon, herring, trout, and other fish. Game, such as quail, wild turkey, and moose, abounded. Plenty of land was available, much of it fertile. A huge supply of timber waited to be harvested, and rich mineral resources had only to be unearthed.

These resources could supply America's needs, and they could also be sold abroad. Overseas markets were eager for Virginia's tobacco, Carolina's rice, and Pennsylvania's wheat. Manufacturing of textiles, tinware, clocks, and glass began to increase. New England shipyards bustled with activity. A steady supply of workers immigrated into the country. America's standard of living in 1789 was high; in some ways, it was already the highest in the Western world.

The position of the United States was promising in other ways too. The young nation was militarily weak compared to France or Great Britain, but at least it was separated from them by a great ocean. While many people had opposed the Constitution, no one—no political party, military group, or potential dictator—had tried to overthrow the republic. Most important, Americans had a growing sense of being one nation. They shared a deep belief in the importance of America's great experiment in government.

Ships brought another important resource into America—a steady supply of immigrant workers—who came to share in America's great experiment in government.

Decisions in the New Government

*G*EORGE WASHINGTON WAS NOT A philosopher of politics as Thomas Jefferson, James Madison, and John Adams were, but certainly he had thought about the subject. In the Virginia House of Burgesses, at the Continental Congress, and later at the Constitutional Convention, he listened to the ideas of many fine political thinkers. By the time he became president, Washington had developed some strong beliefs about government. He wrote no books and made few speeches, but his reports as commander in chief and his correspondence reveal many of those beliefs.

Washington believed in a strong central government. Under the Articles of Confederation, the colonies had each acted almost like independent coun-

Federal Hall in New York, where Washington had been inaugurated, became the seat of the first national government.

Washington, *above,* served with John Adams, *below,* as vice president.

tries. Washington believed they needed to act together. He wrote, "Thirteen sovereignties pulling against each other and all tugging at the foderal [sic] head will soon bring ruin on the whole." Few Americans of Washington's time put the national interest above that of their home state as much as Washington did. He thought "continentally." He wrote, "Let prejudices, unreasonable jealousies and local interest yield to reason and liberality. Let us look to our national character."

When Washington became president, he believed one of his most important tasks would be to make people loyal to the new, national government. He set out to accomplish this in several ways. He traveled around the country—from Georgia to Maine. His visits made the national government more visible and real to people. He chose virtuous men for top positions. He established policies that encouraged trade and investment. And when differences arose, he pressed for compromise, discouraging rivalries between different areas and different types of people. He wanted the states to become one nation.

And he believed that nation should be a republic, with its government in the hands of the people. Few Americans were as strongly against the idea of America having a king as Washington—the man who could have made himself a king. A year or so before the Constitutional Convention, he wrote to John Jay that even talking about becoming a monarchy would be "a triumph for our enemies."

Washington wasn't a "man of the people." He was much more distrustful of the people's judgment than Thomas Jefferson was. He recognized some of the weaknesses of human nature—greed, self-interest, and shortsightedness. He knew that a republic could only survive if its people proved themselves worthy of their liberty. He believed that the great American experiment—that people, left to their own devices, could govern themselves—was important to all humankind. It was worth all his effort to support it.

Washington was also a great believer in freedom of religion. He wrote the Baptists of Virginia that "no one would be more zealous than myself" to protect believers from "the horrors of spiritual tyranny." To the small Jewish congregation in Newport, Rhode Island, he wrote, "Happily the Government of the United States which gives bigotry

Washington helped to unify the new nation. In this engraving, the 13 colonies are ringed around him—"the hub of the union."

no sanction…requires only that those who live under its protection should demean themselves as good citizens."

Washington also believed that America needed time. Every year the government survived was a year for stability, prosperity, and the spirit of nationalism to grow. To gain those years, the nation needed peace. For that reason, Washington felt strongly that America should avoid getting entangled in a European war—so long as this could be done with honor. As he wrote to Patrick Henry in 1795, the best way to do this was "to keep the United States free from political connections with every other country. To see that they may be independent of all and under the influence of none."

Washington confided his hopes for the new government to a dear friend, the French nobleman Marquis de Lafayette.

Washington had fought alongside a young French nobleman, the Marquis de Lafayette, during the Revolution. Washington loved him as a son. Washington wrote to Lafayette just before he became president, predicting that America would prosper, and that Americans would give the credit to their remarkable form of government:

> When the people shall find themselves secure under an energetic government; when foreign nations shall be disposed to give us equal advantages in commerce from dread of retaliation…and when everyone (under his own vine and fig tree) shall begin to taste the fruits of freedom; then all these blessings (for all these blessings will come) will be referred to the fostering influence of the new government.

Setting Up the New Government

Once Washington was inaugurated, he needed Congress to get the new government started. At its first

The first Congress. Congress helped Washington get the new government going.

session in 1789, Congress created three departments—the Departments of State, Treasury, and War—that would be under Washington in the executive branch of the government. Congress also created the position of attorney general. The attorney general and the heads of the departments, who were known as cabinet secretaries, made up the president's cabinet.

The Department of State was responsible for managing foreign affairs, but also for taking the census, granting patents for inventions, and granting copyrights for written materials. The Department of War had responsibility for the army, for establishing a navy, and for relations with Native Americans. The

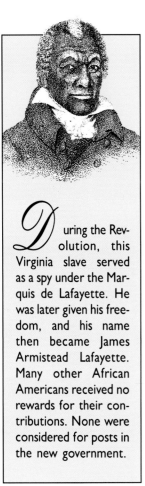

*D*uring the Revolution, this Virginia slave served as a spy under the Marquis de Lafayette. He was later given his freedom, and his name then became James Armistead Lafayette. Many other African Americans received no rewards for their contributions. None were considered for posts in the new government.

Department of the Treasury was by far the largest department. It oversaw the finances of the United States, collecting taxes and customs duties (taxes on goods brought in from foreign countries). In addition, it supervised mail service, until the Post Office Department was created in 1795.

In the judicial branch, Congress established the Supreme Court, which included six justices, as well as a system of lower federal courts. Congress also recommended 12 amendments to the Constitution. Eventually 10 were ratified by the states. On December 15, 1791, these amendments became part of the Constitution—the Bill of Rights.

Washington needed good, able people to fill the new offices created by Congress. He wanted the government to include the "first characters" of the Union—the best politicians and lawyers in each state, people who had distinguished themselves in the Revolution or after. At this time, no women, African Americans, or Native Americans held office anywhere in the United States. Washington did not consider any for office in the national government.

Washington appointed only men he knew, or men who were recommended by someone he knew, so he could be sure of their integrity. He only appointed supporters of the Constitution. Washington wouldn't appoint anyone related to him (he turned down his nephew, Bushrod Washington, as U.S. district attorney for Virginia). He wouldn't accept anyone known to be lazy or a heavy drinker.

Washington made sure that he chose people from all over the country to serve in the executive branch. Since he came from the South and Vice President John Adams came from New England, Washington appointed other high officials from other regions. For example, he chose Alexander Hamilton, who came from a Middle Atlantic state, to head the Department of the Treasury.

Washington also kept that kind of balance when he appointed the chief justice and the five associate justices to the Supreme Court. By his appointments to federal offices throughout his two terms, Washington increased confidence in the new government. He brought a group of men into the government from all over America who set a high standard for honesty and efficiency.

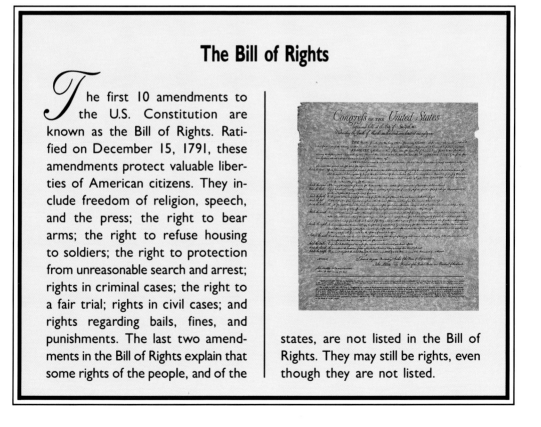

The Bill of Rights

*T*he first 10 amendments to the U.S. Constitution are known as the Bill of Rights. Ratified on December 15, 1791, these amendments protect valuable liberties of American citizens. They include freedom of religion, speech, and the press; the right to bear arms; the right to refuse housing to soldiers; the right to protection from unreasonable search and arrest; rights in criminal cases; the right to a fair trial; rights in civil cases; and rights regarding bails, fines, and punishments. The last two amendments in the Bill of Rights explain that some rights of the people, and of the states, are not listed in the Bill of Rights. They may still be rights, even though they are not listed.

Washington often wore black velvet clothes when he entertained.

Washington's Presidential Style

As soon as the new government had started, Washington needed to make some decisions about how the president should appear to the people. Almost everybody hoped that respect for the president would help unify the country. But what kind of image would ensure that respect? What kind of title should the president be given? What kind of entertaining should he do? Should he travel in a royal or modest style?

Washington turned to Congress for advice on the question of a title. The Senate, led by Vice President John Adams, wanted to give the president a grandiose title. One suggestion was "His Highness the President of the United States of America and Protector of the Rights of the Same." Adams worried that the Constitution had created too weak an executive. A grand title would encourage Americans—and foreign nations—to view the president with awe. Without it, said Adams, the president might be mistaken for the president of a fire company—or a cricket club!

The House of Representatives, led by James Madison, took the opposite view. A majority of the House believed that the president of a republic shouldn't imitate the customs of a kingdom. An elaborate title could even lead to monarchy. After weeks of debate, the House of Representatives won. To this day, the president is announced simply as "The President of the United States."

Washington also wondered how he should entertain. Lavish banquets and dances were an important part of royal courts in Europe. Even in America, governors and mayors often held dinners and fireworks displays to honor important visitors, or simply as entertainment. Washington wanted to do as people wished, but he wasn't quite sure what that was. How could he satisfy the public's need for ceremony without acting like a king?

Washington visited every part of the country as president. On these trips, he often used this carriage.

Ten days after he was inaugurated, Washington wrote to three top advisers—John Adams, John Jay, and Alexander Hamilton. He asked them what they thought the president's conduct should be. He wanted good advice, because he knew he would be setting a precedent for later presidents. He wrote, "Many things may have great and durable consequences from their having been established at the commencement of a new general government."

Washington finally decided to host several kinds of entertainment every week. On Tuesdays, he held dignified levees, or receptions, which any respectably dressed man could attend. On Thursdays, he invited government officials and their families to formal dinners. And on Fridays, Martha Washington invited ladies as well as gentlemen to informal tea parties. The president usually attended Martha's tea parties—and probably enjoyed them most of all.

Washington often looked uncomfortable at the levees. He wore gloves and black velvet clothes, and he carried a cocked hat. Instead of shaking hands with visitors, as presidents do now, he bowed as each guest was presented to him. All of this entertainment cost Washington more than $10,000 each year—twice as much as Vice President John Adams was paid in a year.

George III. Americans wanted their president's style to be different from their former king's.

When Washington visited Congress, he arrived in royal style. He rode in a cream-colored coach drawn by six white horses. Two aides rode with him, and two more followed on white horses. The coaches of the department heads completed the impressive procession.

Washington may have enjoyed such elegance and ceremony. Yet it also had a purpose. It made the president appear to be above ordinary politics, a symbol the nation could respect. This was an important goal of Washington's. Being dignified came naturally to him. He hoped his personal dignity, together with the dignity of these ceremonies and entertainments,

Martha Washington stood on a dais, *left,* at this elegant reception. The president *(in the background)* was criticized by some for "wearing the rags of royalty."

would become attached to the presidency. Later in his presidency, Washington would be violently criticized for wearing the "rags of royalty." But on the whole, his plan succeeded.

How Washington Made Decisions

*E*VEN BEFORE WASHINGTON WAS sworn in as president, he was used to making decisions. He made many during his years as commander in chief and as head of Mount Vernon. Some of those decisions had had a lasting effect on the country. He'd decided to oppose the revolt at Newburgh, keeping the armed forces out of politics. He'd decided to attend the Constitutional Convention, winning it popular support and eventually helping to get the Constitution ratified. His decision to accept the presidency helped win acceptance of the new government. During his two terms as president, Washington made some of the most important decisions ever made by an American president. How did he go about making these decisions?

First, he worked long hours on a regular schedule. He could maintain this pace because of his great

This chamber in Federal Hall housed the nation's first Senate.

75

The Making of a Capital

When Washington became president, the United States did not have a permanent capital city. New York City was chosen as a first, temporary site. In 1791, the capital was moved to Philadelphia. But our nation's founders dreamed of a completely new federal city for the new country.

Several states offered to donate land for a capital. But Congress could not decide whether the capital should be in a northern or a southern state. Then in 1790 Thomas Jefferson and Alexander Hamilton decided on a plan. Jefferson was from the South; Hamilton was from the North. Jefferson agreed to raise support for a bill that Hamilton and other northerners wanted Congress to pass. In return, Hamilton promised to urge congressmen from the North to vote for a U.S. capital in the South.

The agreement worked. Congress asked President Washington to pick the capital's exact location. He chose 10 square miles of farmland and forest on the Potomac River. The new capital city would be called Washington, after the president.

Pierre Charles L'Enfant, an architect, designed the new city. George Washington never lived in Washington, D.C.; the city was not ready until 1800, after he retired as president. It is one of the few cities in the world that was completely planned before it was built.

stamina. Except for two dangerous, month-long illnesses, his health was good during his presidency, and his energy level remained high. He was away from the capital (which was moved from New York to Philadelphia a year and a half after he was inaugurated) just 181 days in eight years (about three weeks a year). The time he was away included his tours of the nation.

An excellent administrator, Washington paid attention to detail. He insisted on knowing about every bit of business handled by the cabinet secretaries. The secretaries made up packets of their mail every day for the president. After reading each packet, Washington returned it, often with questions. Or he discussed it with the department head, sometimes over breakfast.

When Thomas Jefferson, Washington's secretary

The site of Washington, D.C., *far left,* in the early 1790s. On September 18, 1793, Washington laid the cornerstone of the U.S. Capitol, *left,* in the new federal city, later named for him.

of state, later became president himself, he testified to the value of Washington's methods:

> By this means he was always in accurate possession of all facts and proceedings in every part of the union...he formed a central point for the different branches; preserved a unity of object and action among them; exercised that participation in the suggestion of affairs which his office made incumbent on him; and met himself the due responsibility for whatever was done.

In both New York City and Philadelphia, everyone in the government lived and worked near one another, so Washington had close, daily contact with

George Washington, *left,* with his first cabinet. It included Henry Knox, secretary of war; Alexander Hamilton, secretary of the treasury; Thomas Jefferson, secretary of state; and Edmund Randolph, attorney general.

the heads of the departments. He approved or disapproved their plans, asked for their opinions, and had them prepare drafts of state papers for his review. He often sent them files, asking them to discuss the material with him or to write to him about it.

Washington wasn't afraid to have men of the greatest ability as his close advisers. Two of the cabinet secretaries he appointed were far more brilliant than he was: Alexander Hamilton, who served as secretary of the treasury until 1795, and Thomas Jefferson, who was secretary of state until 1793. Washington also sought advice early in his presidency from Chief Justice John Jay, who was without peer in his knowledge of foreign affairs, and James Madison, who was probably the leading figure in the House of Representatives.

Unlike many later presidents, Washington had no problem listening to different views. He encouraged independent ideas and never punished his advisers for their opinions. Still, they all knew who was boss. All major decisions were Washington's. No matter of importance was decided without his approval.

Washington was systematic, orderly, energetic, and insistent on knowing the facts. He was so involved with the work of the Departments of State and War that he was practically his own secretary of state and secretary of war.

Things were different at the Department of the Treasury. Washington knew less about financial matters than he knew about matters of state and of war. But he had chosen a remarkable secretary—Alexander Hamilton—to lead this department. Hamilton's advice to Washington helped put America on a firm financial footing, both at home and abroad.

Alexander Hamilton, Washington's secretary of the treasury, helped put the United States on a firm financial footing.

Hamilton's Financial Program

*A*lexander Hamilton was the genius behind one of the greatest accomplishments of Washington's presidency—making America financially stable. Hamilton knew that people who don't pay their bills have trouble borrowing money. People who repay their loans can get more loans: they have good credit. Hamilton applied this simple truth to the nation. He knew a nation needed good credit in order to prosper. It needed to pay its bills in order to be respected by other nations.

Hamilton was a bold man—impatient, energetic, ambitious, and brilliant. He recommended that the new government pay off all the debts of the American Revolution. He said it should pay not only the national debts, but those of the state governments as well. He proposed methods for how those debts should be paid, including levying the earliest national taxes. And he urged the creation of a national bank.

Hamilton lobbied hard in the Congress to get his program passed. In the end, he didn't get everything he wanted. But many of his ideas were accepted, and they greatly helped the new government. Hamilton's program helped foreign nations and American business leaders see that the new nation would be financially responsible.

United States currency 1793–1796

When Washington needed advice in the early years of his presidency, he talked with one person at a time, or he asked each adviser to write down his views for him. But on November 26, 1791, Washington called his cabinet secretaries to meet together to advise him. This was the first cabinet meeting.

Washington's cabinet met twice that year and three times the next. But in 1793, the nation faced grave foreign policy problems, and the cabinet met 46 times. At these meetings, Washington didn't usually debate with his department heads. Instead, he simply listened and learned.

Washington absorbed what he heard, then made up his own mind. He was independent and impartial in making decisions—just as he was in all his conduct as president. John Adams, himself one of the most independent of men, wrote, "No man, I believe, has influence with the President. He seeks information from all quarters, and judges more independently than any man I ever knew."

Washington was slow and cautious in deciding, both because his mind worked that way, and because he was convinced that the nation's future was at stake. As Alexander Hamilton wrote, Washington "consulted much, pondered much, resolved slowly, resolved surely."

Slowness in making up one's mind was not a flaw in Washington's day. He usually didn't need to react quickly, because most problems were long-term. Travel and communication were slow, so it took time for a crisis to develop. Though Washington was slow to make a decision, once he did he was firm in seeing that it was carried out.

Growing Pains

*W*ASHINGTON RESPECTED THE ROLE of the other branches of government. He never tried to take more power for the presidency than the Constitution allowed—nor did he permit less. He said, "My aim has been and will continue to be neither to stretch nor relax [presidential powers] in any instance whatsoever, unless imperious circumstances render the measure indispensable."

Washington followed the work of Congress carefully—he even asked for copies of each printed bill. But he didn't try to influence Congress, and he refused to support any candidate for Congress. He made only a few proposals to Congress (they were usually accepted). He didn't veto laws simply because he didn't like them, but only when he thought they

After Philadelphia became the nation's capital, some of the daily work of government was carried out at Independence Hall, where the Constitution had been created.

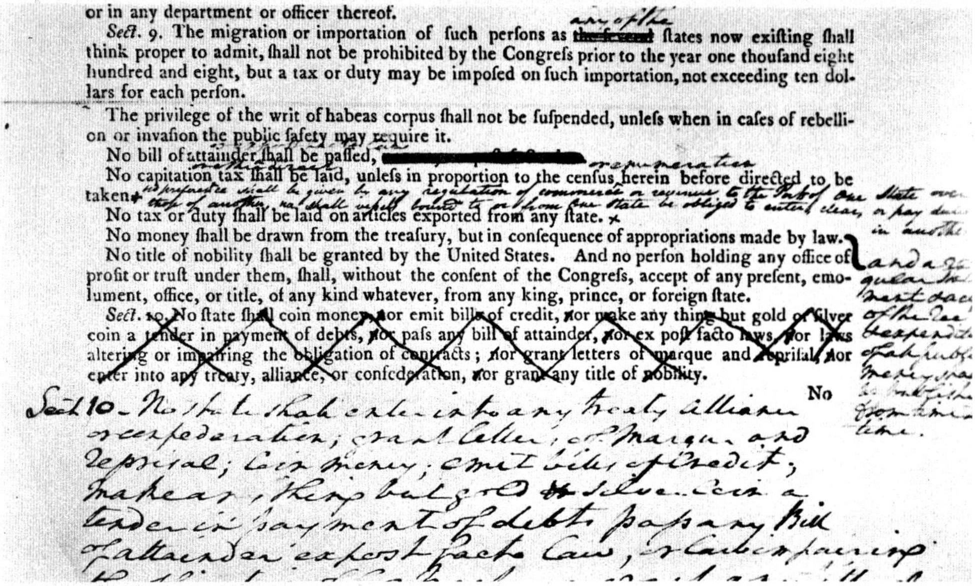

or in any department or officer thereof.

Sect. 9. The migration or importation of such persons as ~~the several~~ states now existing shall think proper to admit, shall not be prohibited by the Congress prior to the year one thousand eight hundred and eight, but a tax or duty may be imposed on such importation, not exceeding ten dollars for each person.

The privilege of the writ of habeas corpus shall not be suspended, unless when in cases of rebellion or invasion the public safety may require it.

No bill of attainder shall be passed,

No capitation tax shall be laid, unless in proportion to the census, herein before directed to be taken.

No tax or duty shall be laid on articles exported from any state.

No money shall be drawn from the treasury, but in consequence of appropriations made by law.

No title of nobility shall be granted by the United States. And no person holding any office of profit or trust under them, shall, without the consent of the Congress, accept of any present, emolument, office, or title, of any kind whatever, from any king, prince, or foreign state.

Sect. 10. No state shall coin money, nor emit bills of credit, nor make any thing but gold or silver coin a tender in payment of debts, nor pass any bill of attainder, nor ex post facto laws, nor laws altering or impairing the obligation of contracts; nor grant letters of marque and reprisal, nor enter into any treaty, alliance, or confederation, nor grant any title of nobility.

[handwritten notes in margins and below]

Washington's copy of the Constitution shows his hand-written notes. In the beginning, the three branches of government struggled to understand what the Constitution intended each of them to do.

were unconstitutional. That happened just twice.

Though Washington didn't try to exercise more or less power than the Constitution granted him, sometimes the Constitution's meaning was not clear. During these early years of interpreting what the Constitution meant, the branches of government sometimes disagreed about what their roles should be.

For example, in 1793 Washington brought an important question to the Supreme Court. Several European nations were at war (including Great Britain and France), and Washington asked the Court what he could do legally—under the Constitution—to keep the United States neutral. But the justices refused to advise him. Courteously but firmly, they told Washington that under the Constitution they couldn't give "advisory opinions." They could only consider questions arising out of lawsuits.

On another occasion, in August 1789, Washington was considering a treaty with the Creek Indians. Since the Constitution said the president "shall have Power, by and with the Advice and Consent of the Senate, to make Treaties," Washington paid the Senate a visit to get the advice. He asked the senators to consider seven points, but they debated each at length. At last, unable to reach agreement, they postponed their vote on each point. Washington is said to have jumped up, red-faced, and said, "This defeats every purpose of my coming here." In the end, the Senate agreed with Washington's views on all seven points. But he never again consulted with the Senate in person.

This incident set a precedent contributing to the balance of powers. The Senate might have turned into a council that advised the president before he made appointments and negotiated treaties. Instead, it now approves appointments after the president has made them and considers treaties after the president has negotiated them. Also during Washington's administration, a precedent was set that the president does not need the Senate's approval to remove people appointed to office in the executive branch. After Washington's administration, the Senate would not try to manage the work of the executive branch.

The Rise of Parties

By the end of Washington's first term, America had changed in many ways. North Carolina and Rhode Island had ratified the Constitution—the last of the original 13 states to do so. Two new states, Vermont and Kentucky, had been admitted to the Union. The first census had been taken. The capital had been

Government officials lived and worked near one another in Philadelphia.

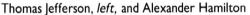

Thomas Jefferson, *left,* and Alexander Hamilton

moved from New York City to Philadelphia, and plans had been made to build a new national capital on the Potomac.

The machinery of government was working well. The government was collecting customs duties, prosecuting lawsuits, registering ships, establishing lighthouses, paying pensions to disabled veterans, and governing the Northwest (the land that included Ohio, Indiana, Illinois, Michigan, and Wisconsin). It would have been a good time for Washington to retire. He thought so and asked James Madison to write a farewell address for him.

But Washington changed his mind. Americans had pulled together for most of Washington's first term. But differences among them began to grow, and many Americans thought that only Washington could keep them all together.

Alexander Hamilton and Thomas Jefferson were at the center of the conflict. They didn't dislike each other, but they disagreed strongly about government policies. Each of them had supporters. The supporters began to split into two camps, which became America's first political parties.

Those who supported Hamilton's policies were called the Federalists. They tended to favor industry, trade, and shipping. The Federalists supported a strong central government with power in the hands of an elite—the richest or most educated people.

Thomas Jefferson's supporters were the Democratic-Republicans, who were generally called Republicans. (Oddly enough, these early Republicans were the ancestors of the present-day Democratic Party.) They were more concerned about the needs of farmers than of businessmen. They worried about the central government becoming too strong. More than the Federalists, the Republicans believed that the people, through their representatives, could be trusted to govern themselves.

Washington valued the advice of both Jefferson and Hamilton. He tried not to take sides with either the Federalists or the Republicans.

Washington tried in every way to be nonpartisan—that is, he tried not to take sides with either party. He wanted to represent the entire nation. Washington feared the "baneful effects of the spirit of party," but he couldn't turn the tide. The differences between the two parties kept growing, and by 1792 they could only agree on one thing. They both wanted George Washington to remain as president. When both sides asked Washington to run again, he agreed. On December 5, 1792, he was unanimously elected president for the second time.

It's hard to understand now why Washington was so upset about the rise of parties. Organized to support certain principles and candidates, political parties have become a permanent part of American politics. They enable Americans to campaign for the things they believe in. But Washington didn't want anything to threaten support for the new government. Americans—including Washington—didn't yet fully understand that opposing the government's policies or opposing the president is not the same thing as disloyalty to the country. Not until the election of 1800, when power passed from the Federalists to the Republicans, did Americans come to understand this. From time to time, we still forget this.

During Washington's second term, party differences became so bitter they seemed to be splitting the country apart. The merchants and bankers of the Northeast rallied behind Hamilton and the Feder-

Differences Between the Parties

FEDERALISTS		REPUBLICANS
Yes	Strong central government	No
Yes	Federal assumption of state debts	No
Yes	Creation of a national bank	No
Yes	Pro-British rather than pro-French	No
Yes	Favor northern business interests	No
No	Favor southern and western farmers	Yes

alists. In the South and West, farmers and working men backed Thomas Jefferson and the Republicans.

As always, Washington tried to stay out of the conflict. He wrote to Jefferson, "I was not a party man myself and the first wish of my heart was, if parties did exist, to reconcile them." But not long after, Jefferson resigned from the cabinet. After Jefferson's resignation, the president began to hear less of the views of the Republicans.

Meanwhile, the Republican party began to sharply attack Washington's policies. Though slow to anger, the president gradually began to side with the Federalists. In a message to Congress in November 1794, he criticized the pro-French Republican societies for playing a part in an uprising called the Whiskey Rebellion. Washington was no longer nonpartisan. He had opened himself up to bitter attack.

During the four years of his second term, Washington made a number of important decisions that helped the new government prosper. But overall, his second term was far less happy than his first. Though he tried, Washington couldn't stop the growth of the parties. Both Jefferson and Hamilton left his cabinet, though he wanted them to stay. In the end, he himself became the target of vicious criticism.

Washington's house in Philadelphia.

The Decision to Put Down the Whiskey Rebellion

ONE OF PRESIDENT WASHINGTON'S most important decisions was to send troops to put down the uprising known as the Whiskey Rebellion. By this action, Washington demonstrated that the national government could enforce its laws and collect taxes—something the government hadn't been able to do under the Articles of Confederation.

In March 1791, Alexander Hamilton asked Congress to place a heavy tax on whiskey to raise money the government needed. Without much objection, Congress agreed. The tax was to be collected from distillers—the makers of whiskey.

Settlers in the West hated this tax. That part of the country (between the Appalachian Mountains and the Mississippi River) hadn't yet developed strong

Washington led 13,000 troops against the Whiskey Rebellion—a show of strength that could not be ignored.

Alexander Hamilton created the hated whiskey tax as one means of raising money for the debt-ridden new government.

ties to the federal government. Western farmers found it expensive to ship their bulky wheat over the mountains to sell it in the East, so they often made the wheat into whiskey, which could be shipped east at less expense. They could also sell the whiskey in the West, or they could trade it for goods. In fact, whiskey was sometimes used in place of money in the West: a one-gallon jug was worth a quarter. Even though the distillers didn't necessarily get cash for their whiskey, they had to pay the tax in cash. And the tax was high—25 percent of the price of a gallon.

One month after the tax went into effect, Washington traveled to western Pennsylvania, to an area that turned out to be the center of resistance to the tax. He stayed at inexpensive inns so he could talk with ordinary people and find out their views about the tax. When he returned to the capital, Washington recommended some changes in the tax, and Congress made them.

But farmers in western Pennsylvania continued to oppose the tax fiercely. The Whiskey Boys, as they came to be called, vowed to prevent collection of the tax. By 1792 they'd rioted in some places. They'd smashed the stills of distillers who paid the tax. They'd even tarred and feathered tax collectors.

Something had to be done. Alexander Hamilton, who had had the idea for the tax, wanted to use force against its opponents. But Washington, as usual, was cautious. He didn't want to use the American army against the American people. Instead, he issued a proclamation, or message, telling the Whiskey Boys "to disperse and retire peacefully." The proclamation said that the rebels had to pay the tax and that the federal government would enforce it.

The Whiskey Boys didn't listen. For the next three years, many of them continued to refuse to pay the tax. Washington let the matter ride. Then, in August 1794, farmers attacked John Neville, a tax inspector, and David Lenox, a federal marshal, as they were serving a summons on a Whiskey Boy. (A summons orders someone to appear in court.) One hundred farmers laid siege to Neville's house. A dozen militia men tried to defend the home, but they were easily overpowered. Neville's house and barn were burned, and Lenox was held captive. Several men were wounded. One Whiskey Boy died.

Washington could not ignore this violence. Hamilton pressed him for action. The rebellion might

FAMOUS WHISKEY INSURRECTION IN PENNSYLVANIA.

Posters in western Pennsylvania cried, "Down with the tax!" while rebellious citizens tarred and feathered a tax collector.

Calling out the Militia

*A*t the time of the Whiskey Rebellion, the United States army was small and its purpose was defense against foreign nations. So Congress passed a law allowing Washington to call out the state militia (an army of volunteers). Several steps had to be taken first, though. A federal judge had to notify the president that a law was being disobeyed. Then the president had to issue a proclamation ordering the rebels "to disperse and retire peacefully." Only then could the president call out the militia.

On August 4, 1794, Washington got his notification from Justice James Wilson. He issued the necessary proclamation after showing it to Thomas Jefferson. He felt "the deepest regret for the occasion." But Washington felt he had no choice; the acts of the rebels amounted to treason.

spread, he argued, and Pittsburgh itself might come under attack. To Hamilton, the strength of the federal government seemed to be at stake. Jefferson, on the other hand, was against taking action.

Washington decided to use force only as a last resort. He met with state officials of Pennsylvania—leaders who were Republicans and hadn't taken the problem seriously. Washington delayed sending troops to the area while these officials negotiated with the rebels. They offered the rebels amnesty, or forgiveness, in exchange for the promise to pay the whiskey tax. But the rebels refused the deal.

By this time, Washington had decided that the federal government must show it could enforce its laws. He decided to send in troops, calling out the militia in the states of Pennsylvania, New Jersey, Maryland, and Virginia. He realized that the states might not want to send troops, since the troops might have to fight their fellow citizens. But Washington needn't have worried. The four states sent almost 13,000 soldiers—far more than he would need.

Though he had more troops than he needed, Washington decided to use all of them. Hamilton had argued that "whenever the government appears in arms, it ought to appear like Hercules and inspire respect by the display of strength."

By the time Washington was ready to use troops, public opinion was on his side. That might not have been true if he had not acted carefully. The giant army began the long hike over the Allegheny Mountains. Washington rode with them—in full military uniform. Never since has an American president led a military expedition. Washington wanted to con-

The Whiskey Boys were mostly farmers in the rolling hills of western Pennsylvania.

trol the organization of the campaign. But he also wanted to show how important he considered this challenge to the federal government.

Also in full uniform with the troops was Alexander Hamilton. Hamilton was temporarily secretary of war (Henry Knox was away in New England). He wanted to march with the army, and Washington allowed it. This was a blunder. Hamilton was the very man responsible for the hated tax. His presence made the episode seem more political, and less a matter of national principle.

Washington rode with the army as far as Bedford, Pennsylvania (about 200 miles west of Philadelphia). Then he left the army under the command of General "Light Horse Harry" Lee. Nearly 5,000 rebels had gathered near Pittsburgh on August 2, and Lee had no idea what he would encounter when his troops reached the area.

General "Light Horse Harry" Lee

But when the army arrived, the Whiskey Boys had almost entirely vanished. Apparently they had decided to do as Washington had asked: "Disperse and retire peacefully." The "rebels" the soldiers did see looked pretty harmless. They were carrying liberty poles (poles striped with red, white, and blue ribbons), not guns. The army took only a handful of prisoners. Eventually, 18 were tried, and 2 were convicted of high treason. Wisely, Washington pardoned both of them.

To some, the huge army's march against the nonexistent rebels seemed ridiculous. Jefferson said sarcastically that the insurrection was "proclaimed and armed against, but could never be found." In fact, Washington may have made a mistake in sending such a huge army against the Whiskey Boys, who

In the end, the Whiskey Boys (seen here with one of their leaders, David Braddock) decided to do as the president had asked: "Disperse and retire peacefully."

were fellow Americans. He definitely should not have let Alexander Hamilton, the creator of the tax, ride along to enforce that tax. In the short run, Washington's use of force against Americans caused many to distrust the Federalists. Still, Washington had dramatically demonstrated the strength of the new government and the loyalty it already commanded.

CHAPTER ELEVEN

The Decision Not to Take Sides in the European War

GREAT WAR SWEPT EUROPE NOT long after Washington became president. In perhaps the most important decision he made as president, Washington determined that the United States should not take sides in it. The European War involved two countries that Americans had strong feelings about—France and Great Britain. For that reason, Washington's decision to stay out of the war caused great controversy.

When Washington became president, most Americans didn't view Great Britain as a friendly nation. Only a few years before, they had fought against the British king and Parliament. On the other hand, France had helped them during the Revolution. The United States and France had even signed an alliance

The French Revolution began as a rebellion against the power of the French king—but ended with the guillotine for thousands of Frenchmen. Other European nations, whose monarchs feared the revolution would spread, soon went to war with France.

Marie Antoinette and Louis
XVI of France

in which the United States promised to help France if Britain attacked French territory in America.

Then in 1789, the French Revolution began, destroying the enormous power of the French king. At first, most Americans had great hopes for the French Revolution. They showed their enthusiasm by singing the "Marseillaise" (the French national anthem) and decorating their hats with tricolor cockades (ribbons of red, white, and blue), as the French revolutionaries did. They called each other "Citizen," in the French revolutionary style. Democratic-Republican societies, or clubs, sprang up to support the French.

After King Louis XVI of France was overthrown, France formed a new government, in which liberal aristocrats would share power with the people. But the liberal aristocrats were soon pushed out of power by mass demonstrations. One group of revolutionaries after another took control of the government. Angry mobs swarmed through the streets, capturing people whom they accused of betraying the revolution. Without fair trials, thousands were executed. Louis XVI himself was executed and so was his queen, Marie Antoinette.

Monarchs in other European nations feared that the revolutionary fever would spread to their countries. In 1791 several of these nations attacked France. Later, France declared war on Spain, Holland, and Great Britain.

Many Americans sang the "Marseillaise" to show their support of the French Revolution. Democratic-Republican clubs also sprang up in support of the revolution. In fact, the French Revolution may have seemed quite similar at first to the American Revolution.

By 1793 France needed help and sought it from its young ally, the United States. France wanted the United States to cooperate in attacking Spanish possessions in North America. France also wanted an advance payment of the money the United States owed it. Finally, France wanted Washington to send a new American diplomat to Paris, one who would be friendlier than Gouverneur Morris, who was U.S. minister to France at the time.

For a while, as the French Revolution progressed, most Republicans in America continued to be pro-French. They disliked the bloodshed, but thought it was justified in overthrowing Louis XVI, whom they considered a tyrant. A new representative of the French Republic, Edmond Genêt (known as Citizen Genêt), traveled around the United States in early 1793, trying to keep enthusiasm high among Americans who supported the French, and raising money and supplies for the French. But as the violence within France grew, and as France went to war with its neighbors, many Americans felt they could no longer support the French.

The Federalists and the Republicans agreed that the United States should stay out of the European War, but it was possible that neither France nor Great Britain would allow that. Washington's policy was to avoid war at a time when the United States was still weak and divided. America could offer little to help either side, and it had much to lose. It would be extremely unwise, Washington said, to enter a war where "our weight could be but small though the loss to ourselves could be certain."

Washington's cabinet agreed in principle that America should remain neutral. But how should it

The storming of the Bastille, a French prison, symbolized French resentment of a monarchy some considered tyrannical.

Citizen Edmond Genêt arrived in America in the spring of 1793 to stir up American support for the French Revolution. He was toasted at many enthusiastic receptions.

achieve that neutrality? Jefferson, for example, wanted to provide France with the "necessaries for war." In other words, he didn't want Americans to fight for the French—but they could send war supplies.

Washington was at Mount Vernon on April 12, 1793, when he received word that France had declared war against its neighbors. He left immediately for Philadelphia. Arriving on April 17, he saw both Alexander Hamilton and Thomas Jefferson the next day. Hamilton brought him a series of questions about neutrality.

Thomas Jefferson had served as United States ambassador to France just before the revolution there began. He sympathized with ordinary French people rather than with the monarchy.

Washington then asked the whole cabinet to consider these questions. Three of the most important were the following: (1) What should the American government do to keep from getting caught in the European War? Should the president issue a proclamation that specifically declared "neutrality"? (2) How should Edmond Genêt be received? (3) Could and should the United States suspend the treaties made with France in 1778? Since the treaties had been made with the French monarchy, were they still valid under the new French government?

The question that needed an immediate answer was the first—how to keep from getting caught in the war. American citizens might commit unneutral acts, such as seizing and burning a British ship in an American harbor. Such an act could plunge the nation into war. The government must take action that would demonstrate the country's neutrality.

Three members of the cabinet—Alexander Hamilton, Henry Knox, and Edmund Randolph—wanted the president to declare America neutral immediately. Thomas Jefferson, on the other hand, argued that such a declaration would be unconstitutional; it was a matter for the Congress. Washington was not convinced by that argument.

But Jefferson also argued that the United States could improve its bargaining power with Great Britain if it did not formally declare neutrality. This second argument did make sense to Washington, and that was what he decided to do.

Three days later, Washington issued a proclamation. He shrewdly avoided declaring the United States "neutral" in the proclamation. Rather, he said the United States would act as "a friendly nation," one at peace with both Great Britain and France. He believed that calling the United States "friendly" to Great Britain might keep the British from attacking American ships or committing other hostile acts. And it warned Americans not to commit acts of war.

Issuing a proclamation is one thing, but holding to it is another. Washington hoped to keep the government as impartial as possible. He personally would be extra careful not to choose sides—even in things he said privately.

On the other hand, his chief advisers felt and acted

Thomas Jefferson was seen by the Federalists as sympathetic to the French Revolution. In this cartoon, Washington is attacking the French while Jefferson tries to stop him.

differently. Hamilton favored neutrality sympathetic to Great Britain; Jefferson favored neutrality sympathetic to France. The two men differed as to whether the treaties of 1778 were in effect and whether the president should receive the new French representative. Washington sided with Jefferson in accepting the treaties as valid, recognizing the new government, and deciding to receive the French diplomat.

That diplomat—the small, ruddy Genêt—caused enormous trouble for Washington. Genêt wanted to use American ports to ready ships to fight in the war for France. He wanted America to supply corn and wheat to the French. And he wanted Americans to fight against the British in Canada and the Spanish in South America. He was encouraged by the enthusiastic reception he got as he traveled around the United States.

When Genêt called on Washington, however, Washington received him coolly. Genêt must have noticed reminders of the alliance between the colonists and the French monarchy, such as the medallions of the French royal family that hung in the room in which he met Washington. And Washington didn't greet him in the French manner—by kissing him on both cheeks and calling him "Citizen."

Rather than welcoming Genêt, Washington told him to order all French ships out of American ports. America couldn't harbor the ships, since that wouldn't be a neutral act. But Genêt defied him. He was so bold that he had a British ship, the *Little Sarah*, brought to Philadelphia after a French ship captured it. After arming the *Little Sarah* with 14 cannon and 120 men, Genêt ordered it to sail as a privateer, or

When Citizen Genêt was presented to Washington, the president received him coolly.

private ship of war, to attack British ships.

Washington didn't want to anger Americans who were pro-French. Nor did he wish to anger the French government. So he waited for Genêt to make an even greater diplomatic blunder. Rumors began to fly about Genêt. One rumor claimed that Genêt had threatened to go over the president's head and appeal directly to the American people to change the policy of neutrality. Another rumor claimed Genêt would demand that Congress choose between Washington and him.

By now even Jefferson thought Genêt was "hot headed, all imagination, no judgment, passionate, disrespectful, and even indecent towards the President." Washington demanded that the French government recall Genêt. He found that it already had. Genêt's friends in the French government had lost power, and the new officials had ordered Genêt's arrest. If Genêt returned to France, he would probably be put to death. Mercifully, Washington allowed Genêt to remain in the United States.

Washington's decision to remain neutral turned out to be wise. By staying out of the European War, Americans gained the time they needed to get used to their new Constitution and for the economy to prosper.

Tensions with France continued for the last 18 months of Washington's administration. The French government even recommended that Washington be overthrown by "the right kind of revolution." By 1794, however, an even greater threat was posed by Great Britain.

Triumph or disaster? Some Americans saw the French Revolution as a triumph for liberty. Others believed it had gone much too far. When Washington refused to join France's war against her neighbors, he lost some friends—and gained others.

The Decision to Back the Jay Treaty

*I*N JUNE 1793, GREAT BRITAIN ORdered its navy to seize any ships taking food to France. Five months later, Britain began to seize all ships sailing to and from the French West Indies. As a result, the British seized some 300 American ships. They also seized many American sailors, forcing them to serve in the British navy. This practice, called impressment, outraged most Americans. Both Republicans and Federalists were shocked. In retaliation, Congress banned trade with Britain for a month and prepared for war by fortifying ports and building warships.

But before going to war, Washington thought peace "ought to be pursued with unremitting zeal." Though a soldier himself, he considered war "the

Fort Detroit was a major center of Indian trade in 1794. The British still occupied it when John Jay set sail for London to negotiate a treaty.

John Jay. Distance made negotiation with foreign nations difficult in Washington's time. Jay signed a treaty with Great Britain in November 1794; Washington received it in March of the next year.

scourge of nations." Washington thought about his options for about a month. He decided to send a diplomat to Great Britain—a special envoy who could try to head off war. But whom should he send, and what should the diplomat's instructions be?

Washington considered sending the man the Federalists wanted—Alexander Hamilton. But finally he chose Chief Justice John Jay. Jay had negotiated with Great Britain before. He and John Adams and Benjamin Franklin had gotten Great Britain to agree to favorable terms in the treaty that ended the American Revolution.

At this time, governments usually gave their diplomats written instructions about what the diplomats could agree to in a treaty. But Jay would be negotiating in faraway London. He would face questions there that neither he nor Washington could possibly foresee. If Jay had to request a change in his instructions, a response might take months to reach him. Washington didn't want to tie the hands of his envoy.

After consulting with his cabinet, Washington decided to give Jay a great deal of freedom. He gave Jay recommendations, not instructions. Jay shouldn't agree to anything that would interfere with America's existing commitments to France. Jay should try to get the British to stop seizing America's ships and sailors. In addition, Jay should encourage the British to allow American ships to dock in the British West Indies, where Americans wanted to sell their surplus crops.

Finally, Washington's envoy was to try to resolve some old business. Great Britain still refused to evacuate its forts in the Northwest. And Americans still owed money to British merchants—debts dating to before the American Revolution.

Jay left New York in May of 1794 and arrived in London about a month later. He signed a treaty for the United States in November, and Washington received it the following March.

Jay's treaty may have been the best that an American envoy could have gotten at the time. It would help avoid war with Britain. At the same time, it didn't violate America's old treaties with France. The British promised to evacuate the forts in the Northwest and agreed to a way to resolve the pre-Revolutionary War debts.

But the Republicans found much to criticize. Jay's treaty failed to win two important concessions. The British hadn't agreed to stop seizing American ships trading with France, nor had they agreed to stop impressing American sailors. In addition, the treaty offered little progress in opening the British West Indies to American trade.

Washington was not pleased with the treaty. It presented him with an enormous political problem. He kept the treaty secret at first, as he considered what to do. Any treaty with the British would have upset the pro-French Americans, but Jay's treaty would outrage them. Yet the alternative could well be war with Great Britain—the world's greatest naval power.

Washington wasn't sure what to do. By now Thomas Jefferson, Alexander Hamilton, and Henry Knox had left his cabinet. Washington turned to his new secretary of state, Edmund Randolph. They decided to send the treaty to the Senate without a recommendation from the president. Under the Con-

Jay Treaty Achievements

Washington's Recommendations

Avoid conflict with U.S. treaties with France	. . . Yes
Get Great Britain to evacuate forts in the Northwest	. . . Yes
Find acceptable way for Americans to repay debts	. . . Yes
Get British to stop seizing American ships	. . . No
Get British to stop impressing American sailors	. . . No
Open U.S. trade with British West Indies	. . . No

stitution, a two-thirds vote of the senators was necessary to approve the treaty. By a vote of 20 to 10, the senators narrowly approved most of it. They refused to approve the section on trade with the British West Indies, however, since it did not grant enough concessions to the United States.

Washington had to decide whether he should complete the ratification process by signing the treaty. Only now did he seek the advice of Alexander Hamilton. Hamilton, with his pro-British leanings, urged ratification. Then Washington received upsetting news. The British, who had voluntarily stopped seizing American ships carrying grain to France, had begun to do so again. The news tipped the balance: Washington would not sign the treaty until the British promised to stop the seizures.

By this time, the Jay Treaty was no longer a secret. Leaked to the press, it aroused outrage. All over the country, it was denounced at mass meetings. When Hamilton tried to make a speech in defense of the treaty in New York, his audience threw stones at him. One mob burned a copy of the treaty on the steps of Jay's house. Other mobs burned dummies of Jay. Indeed, some said Jay could have walked across America in the dead of night, finding his way by the light of these fires.

In the end, Washington pondered the matter alone. He feared war with Great Britain more than war with France. Aware that he might destroy his nonpartisan image, he decided to follow the Senate's advice. He ratified the treaty, except for the section on the British West Indies, but at the same time he protested the British policy of seizing American ships.

*E*dmund Randolph, who had been attorney general, became secretary of state when Thomas Jefferson resigned. He advised Washington about the Jay Treaty.

John Jay was burned in effigy by mobs, angry at the concessions in his treaty.

He got results—the British stopped the seizures. But Washington's decision to ratify the treaty led to another storm of criticism. Once again mobs marched in torchlight processions and burned copies of the treaty. A critic scrawled a message on the house of a treaty supporter in Boston: "Damn John Jay! Damn everyone that won't damn John Jay! Damn everyone that won't put lights in his windows and sit up all night damning John Jay!!''

The fight against the Jay Treaty continued at the capital too. The Constitution seemed to have given the president and the Senate the right to make treaties, and both had ratified the Jay Treaty. But both the Senate and the House of Representatives had the authority to approve money needed for a treaty to go into effect.

Republican leaders in the House opposed the Jay Treaty, and they refused to allocate funds for it. Claiming the right to participate in the treaty-making process, the House asked Washington to submit documents relating to the negotiation of the treaty. The issue had shifted. The real question now, Washington believed, was not whether the Jay Treaty "was a good or bad one, but whether there should be a treaty at all without the concurrence of that House."

Washington refused to give the House of Representatives the documents. He said the framers of the Constitution had a good reason for entrusting treaties to the Senate, the smaller house of Congress. Caution and secrecy were important in such negotiations, so it was better to have fewer legislators involved. The argument barely carried the day. In the end, the House appropriated the money by a narrow vote of 51 to 48.

Washington signed the Jay Treaty knowing it would create political havoc for him—and for the country.

Washington had steered the nation through another crisis. He made a number of important decisions about the Jay Treaty. He sent John Jay as a special envoy to Great Britain and gave Jay freedom to negotiate. He let the Senate vote on the treaty without his recommendation and then ratified the

This scene is part of a map of early Virginia. American goods could be shipped from wharves such as this one to ports around the world. Seeking new markets, Americans wanted the Jay Treaty to open the British West Indies to American trade.

treaty. And he didn't give in to the House of Representatives. Taken together, these decisions helped keep the United States out of war with Great Britain for almost 20 years.

America received another bonus from the Jay Treaty. Spain believed the Jay Treaty would bring closer relations between the United States and Great Britain. Worried about being isolated, Spain hastened to negotiate its own treaty with the United States, agreeing to quite favorable terms. In fact, the Pinckney Treaty opened the entire Mississippi River to American traffic. Americans could use the vital port of New Orleans for three years, and could renew the agreement beyond that time.

Washington was able to keep the United States out of war with the major European powers during his two terms. He did this by deciding the United States should remain neutral and then by firmly implementing that policy. The United States was thus spared probable military disasters, economic difficulties, and possibly even civil war. In 1795 John Quincy Adams gave credit where it was due:

> If our neutrality be still prevented, it will be due to the President alone. Nothing but his weight of character and reputation, combined with his firmness and political intrepidity, could have stood against the torrent that is still tumbling with a fury that resounds even across the Atlantic.

Peace isn't always the most popular policy in the short run, however. Washington's foreign policy hurt his popularity. He became the subject of bitter personal attacks during his second term. In fact, he was criticized as viciously as any president in our history. Republican newspapers called him "an imposter," the "most horrid swearer and blasphemer," and "the man who is the source of all the misfortunes of our country." Indeed, during Washington's second term, the Republican press approved of only one of his decisions—his decision to retire.

In the end, the Jay Treaty helped ensure peace, made the seas safer for American sailors, and triggered a favorable treaty with Spain.

CHAPTER THIRTEEN

The Decision to Step Aside

*M*AKING THE DECISION NOT TO seek a third term wasn't hard for Washington. He hadn't even wanted a second term. Four years later, he had aged greatly. The last few years of his presidency also cost him dearly in reputation.

Though not difficult to make, the decision to step aside was an important one. Washington was anxious to set a precedent of succession to the presidency. A president shouldn't retain power for life, but rather should pass it on to another person chosen in a free election. Washington wanted to give "an early example of rotation in an office of so high and delicate a nature." Such an example would be in "accord with the republican spirit of our Constitution and the ideas of liberty and safety entertained by the people." Had Washington died in office, Americans

Americans regretted the loss of George Washington when he stepped down as president and mourned him, two years later, when he died. This memorial parade took place in Philadelphia.

Washington's "Farewell Address" defended Federalist policies. It may have helped Federalist John Adams win the presidency in 1796.

might never have known that power meant less to Washington than this "republican spirit."

The way Washington announced his retirement is also important. He combined the announcement with a statement of his political philosophy. It was published as his "Farewell Address" in Philadelphia's *Daily American Advertiser* on September 17, 1796—three months before the presidential election. It was never given as a speech.

In it, Washington offered his advice to his countrymen as "an old and affectionate friend." He urged them not to be swept up by party fervor, and warned them against "the mischiefs of foreign intrigue." Hailing the Constitution, he said true liberty lay in "respect for its authority, compliance with its laws, acquiescence in its measures."

The most important message in the "Farewell Address" concerned foreign policy. Permanent "antipathies against particular nations and passionate attachments for others" should be avoided, he wrote. Washington wasn't urging Americans to isolate themselves from the rest of the world. But he was warning against too much love or too much hate of any foreign country.

Washington was reemphasizing his policy of neutrality—one that had guided many of his foreign policy decisions. His advice was simple: "Observe good faith and justice toward all nations. Cultivate peace and harmony with all." The "Farewell Address" expressed a farsighted understanding of the American national interest. It became the basis for American foreign policy for more than 100 years.

Washington's "Farewell Address" was a justification of his policies and those of the Federalists. It may have helped Federalist John Adams win his razor-thin victory over Thomas Jefferson in the presidential election of 1796. Washington didn't campaign for Adams, but he must have been pleased by his victory.

The race between Adams and Jefferson was bitter. But when it was over, nobody plotted to take over the government. Nobody rebelled. Once again, Washington helped make possible a peaceful transfer of power, just as he had at the end of the American Revolution and at the end of government under the Articles of Confederation. This time he set a precedent for our presidential succession process, "one of the miracles of the American constitutional system."

Washington went alone, on foot, to the inauguration of John Adams. One onlooker recalled the

Washington toasted John Adams at a farewell dinner.

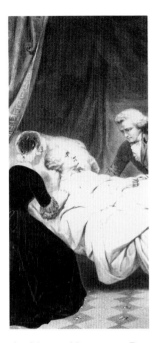

At Mount Vernon in December 1799, George Washington's life came to an end.

jubilation of the crowd when Washington arrived. "No sooner was his person seen, than a burst of applause such as I had never before known, and which it would be impossible for one to describe, saluted the venerable Hero and Patriot."

John Adams himself wrote: "A solemn scene it was, indeed: and it was made more affecting to me by the presence of the General whose countenance was as serene and unclouded as the day....All agree that, taken together, it was the sublimest thing ever exhibited in America."

The great nineteenth-century writer Washington Irving described Washington's experience that day. "There was a rush from the gallery to the corridor, so eager were the throng to catch a last look of one who had so long been the subject of public veneration....The crowd followed him to his door. There, turning around, his countenance assumed a grave and almost melancholy expression, his eyes bathed in tears, his emotions too great for utterance, only by gestures could he indicate his thanks and convey his farewell blessing."

Last Years

Washington returned to Mount Vernon in 1797. Though he was just 65, he was a tired, old man. He may have been glad, finally, to "sit under his vine and fig tree." Surprisingly, though, his service to the country wasn't over.

Within a year, an undeclared war at sea with France was under way. President Adams needed to prepare an army to defend America, should France decide to invade. Before even consulting Washington, Adams appointed him as commander in chief, and

Washington accepted. Washington appointed men he trusted—including Alexander Hamilton and Henry Knox—as his top generals. Together, they laid plans to defend America. However, a formal declaration of war between the two countries was never made, and Washington never actually needed to raise an army.

Many of our country's founders enjoyed long lives. John Adams lived to be 90, James Madison to be 85, Benjamin Franklin to be 84, and Thomas Jefferson and John Jay to be 83. Washington was just 67 when he ventured out one cold December night to inspect his farms. A snowstorm blew up, and he rode home. The next day he had a sore throat, but his condition worsened over the next two days. Late in the evening of December 14, 1799, with Martha Washington beside him, George Washington's life came to an end.

Leaders of True Nobility May Come to Power

Americans have honored George Washington in many ways. The nation's capital is named for him. So is one state and many counties, towns, and villages. His face appears on the United States quarter and the one-dollar bill. It's even carved in the famous national monument at Mount Rushmore. Should Washington be held in such esteem?

Americans of Washington's day had many reasons to honor him. He held an army together against heartbreaking difficulties, and then prevented the army from becoming a force in American politics. He used his great prestige to convince his countrymen to replace the Articles of Confederation. After

The nation's capital is named for Washington.

At his death, Washington was pictured godlike, ascending into heaven. Washington was not a god but a man who made mistakes, as well as many wise decisions.

heading the Constitutional Convention, he allowed his reputation to be used to help get the Constitution ratified. His support of the Constitution was a major reason it was accepted by all Americans within a few years.

As president, Washington got the government started with energy, dignity, and honesty, and he inspired confidence in it. While respecting the other branches of government, he acted decisively within the powers granted to the president by the Constitution. He found men of genius to advise him—

men of strong and conflicting views. Together, their vision made the United States financially secure and kept the country out of a great European war. Under Washington, the United States government came to command respect for its integrity and competence.

Washington's presidency ended in a mess of party bitterness. The Republicans openly criticized the Federalists, who were in power. Though Washington hated criticism, he helped insure that, in America, criticism would not be considered treason. By voluntarily stepping down from office, he reinforced the understanding that the president would not be a king, but that in America we choose our government by election.

Courageous but cautious, dignified but shrewd, Washington continues to be a model of leadership. His life demonstrates that leaders of true nobility may come to power, rule wisely, remain uncorrupted, and return to private life unspoiled. This is, as historian Marcus Cunliffe has written, "an achievement still to be marveled at and never to be taken for granted." Washington died knowing that he had bought time for the great republican experiment he believed in so deeply. He bought America the time it needed, knowing well that time was on its side.

Washington's face appears on the U.S. quarter—one of many ways in which he is remembered. The living man was courageous and dignified—a leader of true nobility.

Index

Acknowledgments

Photographs reproduced with permission of: Independence National Historical Park, pp. 6, 14, 65, 86 (both); National Archives, pp. 8 (above), 12, 17, 36, 37, 44, 53, 66, 71, 79, 104, 120; IPS, pp. 8-9 (below), 11, 48, 64 (both), 81, 89, 92, 125 (above); Mount Vernon Ladies Association, pp. 15, 19, 22; St. John's Lodge, No. 1, New York City, p. 16 (below); Library of Congress, pp. 3, 16 (above), 18, 20, 21, 25, 29, 33, 38, 40, 46, 49, 52, 56, 69, 70, 74, 76, 78, 79, 84, 85, 100 (both), 102, 103, 110, 113, 114, 121, 122; Washington and Lee University, Lexington, Virginia, pp. 24, 35; Red Hill, The Patrick Henry National Memorial, Brookneal, Virginia, p. 27; Metropolitan Museum of Art, pp. 28, 90; Kennedy Galleries, Inc., New York, p. 30; Sons of the Revolution in the State of New York, Headquarters, Fraunces Tavern, New York City, p. 32; Architect of the Capitol, p. 34; New York Public Library, Emmet Collection, p. 41; American Antiquarian Society, pp. 42-43; The Virginia Museum of Fine Arts, Gift of Colonel and Mrs. Edgar W. Garbisch, p. 45; The Bettmann Archive, pp. 50, 67, 93, 101, 106, 107; National Museum of American History, Smithsonian Institution, p. 51; Abby Aldrich Rockefeller Folk Art Center, Williamsburg, Virginia, p. 54; Maryland Historical Society, pp. 57, 116; New Hampshire Historical Society, p. 117; Houghton Library, Harvard University, p. 60; Massachusetts Historical Society, p. 61; Collection of the New-York Historical Society, pp. 62, 105; Virginia Historical Society, p. 68; National Portrait Gallery, London, p. 72; The Brooklyn Museum, Huntington's "Republican Court" (detail), p. 73; John D. Melius, by permission of The Supreme Council, 330, Scottish Rite of Freemasonry, S.J., USA, p. 77; Smithsonian Institution, p. 80; Library Company of Philadelphia, pp. 82, 118; Virginia State Library and Archives, pp. 87, 96; Ray W. Forguer, Washington, Pennsylvania, pp. 95, 97; Mansell, p. 98; Burton Historical Collection, Detroit Public Library, p. 108; New York Public Library, p. 115; Gene Ahrens, p. 123; Huntington Library, p. 124; Cleveland Museum of Art, p. 125 (below).

Back cover: Independence National Historical Park